# FLUXUS

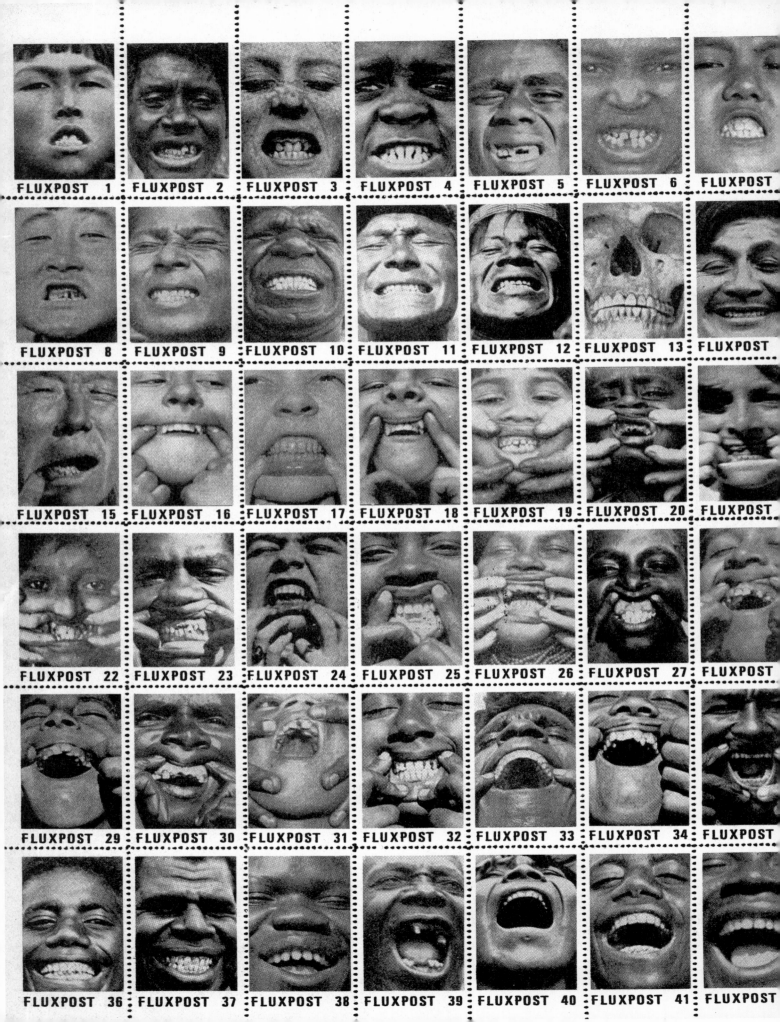

Thomas Kellein

# FLUXUS

Thames and Hudson

The author wishes to acknowledge Corinne Baier, Jon Hendricks and Hanns Sohm for their most valuable assistance.

Frontispiece: GEORGE MACIUNAS **Fluxpost** (Smiles), 1978, Fluxus Edition, 28 x 22 cm (s. no. 124)

First published in Great Britain in 1995
by Thames and Hudson Ltd, London
First published in the United States of America in 1995
by Thames and Hudson Inc., 500 Fifth Avenue, New York, New York 10110
© 1995 Kunsthalle Basel and the photographers

Photographs:
The Gilbert and Lila Silverman Collection: Cover (front and back), pp. 8, 13, 20, 30, 31 right, 32, 34, 35, 38 bottom, 39, 46, 47, 61-65, 68, 70, 71, 73, 77 top, 80-83, 87-89, 91 top, 94-96, 97 top, 100 right, 101-104, 105 top, 108-110, 117, 121, 127-129, 135. Private collection: Frontispiece, pp. 6, 17, 28, 29, 31 left, 38 top, 40 left, 49, 51-53, 57-59, 67 top, 74, 76, 78, 79, 90, 92, 98, 99, 105 bottom, 106, 111. Archiv Sohm, Staatsgalerie Stuttgart (Franziska Adriani/Andreas Freytag/Hartmut Rekort): pp. 33, 40 right, 41-45, 48, 50, 54, 55, 66 67 bottom, 69, 72, 77 bottom, 84-86, 91 bottom, 93, 97 bottom, 100 left, 107, 112-116. Collection Onnasch (Lothar Schnepf): pp. 36, 37.

British Library Cataloguing-in-Publication Data
A catalogue record for this book is available from the British Library
ISBN 0-500-97422-5
Library of Congress Catalog Card Number: 95-60188

Edited by Thomas Kellein and Jon Hendricks
Layout by Hansjörg Mayer
Printed in Germany by Staib + Mayer, Stuttgart

# Table of contents

**Thomas Kellein**
**I make jokes! Fluxus Through the Eyes of "Chairman"**
**George Maciunas**                                                  7


**Selected Works**                                                   27


**Jon Hendricks**
**Uncovering Fluxus – Recovering Fluxus**                           119


**Bibliography**                                                    139

| Cynthia Boeke treble viol | Walt McKibben base viol cotra-baseviol counter tenor voice | Max Serbin treble and tenor viol |
| Stanley Buetens tenor lute, recorder tenor voice | Kent Salisbury s.a.t.b. recorders soprano krummhorn bass voice | Brian D. Stewart alto trombone |
| D.Young Chung soprano sordun tenor recorder tenor krummhorn | Ephraim Segerman alto, tenor lute theorbo, vihuela tenor viol | Howard Vogel alto dulcian tenor krummhorn s.a.t.b. recorders |
| Philip Corner tenor trombone | Don Smithers Musical Director base sordun base krummhorn sopranino, s.a.t.b. recorders & cornetto | Ralph Zeitlin alto krummhorn alto recorder cornetto |
| Sonia Gezairlian harpsichord percussion | Instrumentation | George Maciunas producer |

Theatrum INSTRuMENTORuM

Thomas Kellein

# I MAKE JOKES!

## Fluxus Through the Eyes of "Chairman" George Maciunas

*"Well, there's a lot, too much high art,*
*in fact, that's why we're doing Fluxus."*
George Maciunas 1978

### The Reality

Was Fluxus what Joseph Beuys did?[1] Is Fluxus an art movement?[2] Is Fluxus beyond all categorisation? "Paradoxically, the details of how Fluxus began seem to become clearer to some historians the further they are in the past," wrote Emmett Williams in 1991. "My own memory gets darker and darker, if what is remembered is true at all."[3] Whether in spite of or because of the Fluxus aversion to definitions, no other art form of the 60s and 70s has spawned such a welter of publications and exhibitions in recent times. More than twenty catalogues and some six different catalogues raisonnés of individual collections have been published in the last ten years, a dozen art magazines have dedicated special issues to the subject and, since 1988, there exists a **Fluxus Codex**, a 600-page encyclopaedia of all the Fluxus editions ever published or planned.[4] The many graduate dissertations and doctoral theses on the subject and the innumerable presentations at various symposia reflect the enormous and almost insatiable curiosity amongst art historians about what Fluxus may have been. In spite of this, Fluxus has still not been included in any museum collection of modern or contemporary art.[5] Nor have the Fluxus multiples, which sold in the 70s at prices of between $2.50 and $150, increased much in value on the art market.[6] It would seem that this subject matter provides part of the art scene with the perfect opportunity for work, and one with which they feel they can fully identify, while major museums and art-historical surveys continue to let the inventory of existing Fluxus works and the wealth of pioneering Fluxus performances fall by the wayside.

Fluxus belongs to that era of economic upturn known in Germany as the years of the *Wirtschaftswunder* and, in the USA, the *Affluent Society*. It was a time of unprecedented prosperity in the industrialised capitalist nations of the Western world, a time of faith in a worldwide consumer society. Even in the arts and in philosophy, until around 1970, people believed in the infinite perfectibility of productive forces.[7] As proof of a seemingly boundless capacity for expansion, the Americans, still reeling from the Sputnik shock of 1957 which brought home

George Maciunas and his mother, Leokadia Maciunas, 1945 at Bad Nauheim

George Maciunas and his sister Nijole 1949 at Levitown, Long Island, New York

to them an awareness of the Soviet Union's space missions, set their sights on being the first to put a man on the moon. That goal was achieved in 1969, a year of student revolt and war in Vietnam. The political face of this decade of innovation was shaped primarily by the "nuclear balance of terror" in the shadow of atomic weapon stockpiling by the USA and the USSR. The "negative" or the "other" in the major industrial nations seemed somehow as distant and intangible as some omnipotent and imageless god.[8]

The task of reflecting the expansive cultural hegemony of the consumer aesthetic with its non-metaphysical promise of happiness fell to Pop Art and, in some respects, to Nouveau Réalisme, but not to Fluxus.[9] Happenings were criticised as harmless in this respect.[10] Though Fluxus products seemed too poor and shabby to make much impression in the affluent society, the press at least reported on the irritation and awkwardness of Fluxus performances.[11] The two dozen or so artists, scattered across several countries, who joined forces to organise concerts and publications between 1962 and 1964 under the name of Fluxus enjoyed a certain *succès de scandale* as avantgardists, attracting vituperative media coverage until well into the early 70s. With few exceptions, however, they were not shown in major art galleries and exhibition spaces until the 80s. Then, having failed to make their mark as generic intermedia or multimedia artists,[12] the makers and shakers of Fluxus were hailed as a group of early postmodernists.[13] At the same time, details of their work and its art-historical "repercussions" were debated as an incomprehensible phenomenon. After all, the Fluxus artist, in so far as one can compare the central figure of George Maciunas with Joseph Beuys or the mature Nam June Paik, was, to put it bluntly, an alarming social failure. In the turbulent change of the 60s, he tended to be overlooked. In the 70s, he failed to have any links with the more thought-provoking project and process art. Before the art boom of the 80s had taken hold, he had died. But then again, there was in any case no volume of early drawings and objects which could have been marketed profitably.

In the eyes of academia, such unmitigated failure may be regarded as the hallmark of those who stand on high moral ground. Indeed, many young art historians seem to savour the systematic complexity of Fluxus, with its flurry of events, venues and aims, like a draught from a fresh spring. Some 33 years after the first Fluxus concerts, there is something seemingly futile about seeking to present Fluxus as a single entity. In order to keep up with the sheer quantity of data painstakingly archived from the very beginning,[14] one must concentrate either on the products or the chronology or on the individuals involved – it is simply not possible to deal with them all together at the same time, unless one takes a rather nostalgic delight in the pursuit of chaos. Maciunas, the founder and main protagonist of Fluxus, never actually succeeded in carrying out his chosen role. This is probably the main reason why any presentation of Fluxus must necessarily remain one-sided. The older artists who were personally involved in most of the important events are not surprised by this. Williams, who in recent years, has often taken the role of a tongue-in-cheek narrator in the flood of art-historical writing about Fluxus, commented on his sense of darkness, quoted above, with a mischievous remark made by his colleague Al Hansen:

*"Be careful with that 'darker and darker' stuff, Emm(...). People might say you've blown a fuse up there."* [15]

All the same, it is easy enough to sketch a rough outline of the history of Fluxus: in the winter of 1960/61, Maciunas, a New York design student of Lithuanian origin, prospective art historian and unsuccessful dealer in antique musical instruments, met some of the young artists and composers grouped around John Cage, and wanted to publish their work in a magazine called **Fluxus**. From 1962 onwards, instead of being involved with the magazine or other Fluxus works in New York, Maciunas began organising Fluxus concerts in a number of European cities, attracting an international following of young artists. Maciunas saw the concerts developing into an organisation which would protect the copyright of the individual artists and successfully market and monopolise their work, building a bulwark of cultural policy against serious art. However, as the intended exclusivity involved insoluble economic problems right from the start and was not even favoured by many of those involved, most of the musicians, writers and artists soon distanced themselves from him. Maciunas continued to pursue his editorial activities undeterred, producing several hundred different Fluxus products by 1978. He continued to aim for a dictatorship of the artistic proletariat, even though Fluxus production depended entirely on him, like a one-man factory.[16]

In the list of names and letters disseminated from Wiesbaden and New York, Maciunas had described himself from the very beginning as the "Chairman" of Fluxus.[17] Particularly esteemed colleagues played the role of disciples and only in moments of crisis did he offer a colleague the function of Co-Chairman.[18] Later, he allocated sovereign territories: **Fluxus-North, Fluxus-South, Fluxus-East** and **Fluxus-West**. But the **HQ** – after its beginnings in 1962/63 at Ehlhalten in Germany's Taunus mountains – remained in New York until a severe attack on Maciunas in 1976 in which he lost an eye. From 1963, from his base in Soho, he drew up lists of artists, wrote letters, distributed pamphlets, placed printing orders and organised the distribution of works through a few middlemen. The aesthetic quality, which he felt was conducive to the "movement" and necessary for the projected editions, was to have a revolutionary effect on cultural policy. Maciunas had very precise ideas of what Fluxus was and how Fluxus should be used to trigger profound change. The motto of the early years was the concept of "concretism". According to an initial manifesto, referring explicity to Dadaism, all *"'time' arts to 'space' arts (with) no borderlines"* were to be subjected to fundamental disillusionment[19] in order to help all genres and consequently the arts in general, to achieve a kind of one-dimensionality. According to the prolific correspondence he later exchanged with almost all his colleagues, this ideal was upheld by George Brecht, Nam June Paik, Ben Vautier, Robert Watts and most notably La Monte Young, in their works. From 1963 onwards, Brecht, Vautier and Watts were willing to supply ideas for the Fluxus multiples which were then issued in small plastic boxes, generally measuring 3 x 12 x 9 cm. The ideas behind the many **Games & Puzzles** boxes by George Brecht, involved, for example, in the case of the **Swim Puzzle**, placing a small shell in a box and printing a card with the words **Swim Puzzle**. Maciunas was inundated with so many reponses to his request that this – and strictly speaking only this – led to the manifestation of the lasting works of Fluxus art. For the performances, the Chairman organised the programmes, wrote the invitations to the artists, designed the posters and leaflets, rented the premises, drew up the performance schedule as far as possible, took photographs, organised accommodation and afterwards considered himself responsible for the production of permanent products by the artists he admired, in the form of the Fluxus boxes. He therefore took it upon himself to organise the necessary objects, he dealt with all the necessary correspondence, wrote the respective cards or scores for the boxes, designed and printed the labels, took care of the distribution of the multiples and eventually founded the **Fluxus** magazine (again, edited and designed by him) as a means of reaching the few potential intermediaries – the Fluxus artists in Europe, keeping them informed and up-to-date with additional price-lists and offers.

The works were simple, small and cheap. With them, an art form emerged which was projected superficially as a gag and a paradox. The entire system of editions was launched with an awareness of the ready-mades by Marcel Duchamp, the boxes by Joseph Cornell and the 1961 exhibition of "The Art of Assemblage" at the Museum of Modern Art, where George Brecht and Robert Watts had presented original works along with many other European and American artists since the Dada era.[20] Fluxus, however, did not seek to criticise high art and continuously expand it. Instead, Maciunas intended to combat and reject the system of high art once and for all, especially its "baroque" tendencies, even within anti-art forms. For example, the standard edition of Ben Vautier's **Mystery Box** was to contain dust. A larger, luxury version measuring 5 x 20 x 20 cm, was to be filled with egg shells. A cube-shaped object measuring 25 x 25 x 25 cm, the **Mystery Box** was to contain garbage: "chipped plaster, used mimeograph stencils, dried up tea bags (used), orange skins, etc.," as he wrote from New York in February 1964, asking Ben's permission and adding, with a certain macabre pragmatism:

> "This will be very practical since we can dispose of garbage by this method and even get money for it."[21]

On grounds of time alone, the idea of systematically destroying the illusions of art was doomed to failure. "Dear Ben," he wrote in another of his protocol-like letters to his colleague Vautier in Nice, "am completely snowed under with work." He described how he was spending eight hours a day on the **Fluxhouse Cooperative**, a further project involving the search for money and tenants to finance the Fluxus artists' lofts in Soho,[22] three hours on an **Implosions Business** to raise money for Fluxus through the sale of stickers, serviettes, table cloths or

T-shirts,[23] four for the magazine **Film Culture** with which he earned his living, three for the Fluxus projects and five for eating and sleeping.[24] Looking back on his permanently precarious financial situation, at the end of his life, he remarked that he had regularly spent about 90 per cent of his entire income on Fluxus, especially on the production of multiples.[25]

Day in and day out, upholding the Fluxus idea demanded stringent economy in his private life: "For food you need $5 per week if you eat like me (Spartan diet)...," he told Ben in 1964 when Ben informed him of his plans to head for New York, as so many artists did, with neither money nor prospects.[26] Apart from the financial difficulties which Maciunas overcame by practising strict asceticism throughout his life, he was dogged by health problems, including severe asthma, and was burdened by the vehement criticism which many Fluxus artists had levelled against the methods and aims of his anti-art programme at an early stage.

For the last major Fluxus concert for some time, held at the Kunstakademie Düsseldorf on 2nd and 3rd February 1963, he had designed a manifesto in which a copy of the dictionary definition of Fluxus, with such concepts as **Purge**, **Tide** and **Fuse**, was commented on with hand written notes to coin a revolutionary strategy against bourgeois art culture.[27] Only in the winter of 1962 had a **Fluxus News Letter** proposed an exclusive contract for the artists then most recently involved in Fluxus, in which Maciunas promised eighty per cent of revenues to the authors.[28] However, there was never any editorial budget nor any concert revenues. The fateful **News-Policy Letter No. 6**, issued on 6th April 1963 after the Düsseldorf manifesto, in which Maciunas outlined propaganda activities for a projected Fluxus festival in New York over a period of several months – involving traffic chaos and disturbance of the press, museums, theatres and concert halls – led to the successive break-up of the artists just nine months after Fluxus had begun in Europe. Robert Morris distanced himself from Fluxus in writing and called for his texts to be deleted from the 1963 edition of **An Anthology**.[29] Walter De Maria, in his "Portrait of the School of Cage, Caged" (1963), published in Fluxus newspaper **ccV TRE** No. 2, left no doubts about his opinion of the internationally active Cage students' concerts and performances.[30] Daniel Spoerri, whose **L'optique moderne** Maciunas had published in 1963 as one of the few Fluxus publications in Europe, wanted no further contact with "Fluxus affairs" as a "professional" artist.[31] Other European artists, most notably Wolf Vostell and Joseph Beuys, recognised their opportunity and simply took Maciunas' works and ideas out of his hands.[32] From New York, the **News-Policy Letter No. 6** elicited a lengthy response of several pages from Jackson Mac Low, co-publisher of the pioneering **An Anthology**, which Maciunas had actually intended to publish before leaving New York. In it, he spoke in favour of high art and its institutions.[33] Dick Higgins, one of the main protagonists in the early performances, expressed his profound displeasure at Maciunas' organisational ineffectiveness and, after breaking with him in the publishing field, even threatened him with legal action.[34]

George Maciunas (standing 2nd from the left) on June 9, 1962, during the "Kleines Sommerfest 'Après John Cage'", Galerie Parnass, Wuppertal (Photo Rolf Jährling)

Given the fact that Maciunas had already spent five months in New York in 1961 attempting unsuccessfully to finance the **Fluxus** magazine through concerts and exhibitions at his AG Gallery, the question arose from the outset as to why, when he was in Germany, he should suddenly voice his intention – on the strength of a few concert performances – of asserting Fluxus as an "anti-professional",[35] primarily social and non-aesthetic political instrument aimed at dismantling high art. In his much-quoted letter to Tomas Schmit in the winter of 1963/64,[36] in which he invoked his vision of a "gradual elimination of fine arts", an anti-individualistic attitude, an anti-European working approach and a total merger of the projected ready-made culture of multiples and performances in daily life, Maciunas had argued in favour of this social goal, even though the insoluble misunderstandings with his colleagues had already become manifestly clear. In March 1964, when he was, to all intents and purposes, left entirely alone with his idea of an artists' collective, he accused Ben Vautier, his most faithful supplier of items apart from Brecht, of "GROWING MEGALOMANIA". In draconian tones he advised:

*"Curb & eliminate your ego entirely (if you can) don't sign anything – don't attribute anything to yourself – depersonalize yourself! That's in true Fluxus collective spirit. Deeuropanize yourself!"* [37]

To the few artists still interested in concerts, he wrote of a projected – albeit financially inconceivable – tour of Asia with Fluxus. La Monte Young, who had selected the items for **An Anthology**, but who had not participated in the European Fluxus concerts of 1962 and 1963, was the first to receive this news in a letter, because he also looked like he was breaking away. Maciunas had not kept his promise of publishing more of his music.[38] Nevertheless, he wrote imperiously from Germany to the composer and musician in New York:

*"Why are you going to India?????? what are you up to? Why not stick around in Europe and then join us on a tour of East Europe and USSR late in 1963??? then settle down in Siberia. Climate there would be very healthy, nice cool winters. Give concerts along the Siberian railroad stops. Think it over."* [39]

## The Illusion

In his last interview, given in 1978, Maciunas replied to the question of whether, perhaps, he saw Fluxus as art after all by saying:

*"No. I think it's good, inventive gags."* [40]

Jonas Mekas, the filmmaker and companion who had known him longest and best because of their continuous work together for **Film Culture**, said in 1992 that the decisive criterion of quality for him, even in film, had always been "fun".[41] In the Fluxus definition for a fold-out in the *Tulane Drama Review* magazine in 1965 it says that Fluxus is a "fusion of Spike Jones, gags, games, vaudeville, Cage and Duchamp."[42]

But what does **Concretism** mean? How did the vision of the gradual dissolution of high art manage to survive for so long even though Maciunas sold hardly any Fluxus products in his lifetime,[43] did not publish the collected works of many artists and generally burdened himself with even more problems in all the follow-up projects intended to finance Fluxus?

The illusion of Fluxus would appear to have some connection with an idea of world art he had already addressed in the 50s. In a brief biography written in 1976, under the heading "Education", he lists three courses of study: 1949-1952 art, graphic art and architecture at the Cooper Union, New York; 1952-1954 architecture and musicology at the Carnegie Institute of Technology, Pittsburgh; and, from 1955-1960, a continuous study of European and Siberian art at the time of the early mediaeval migration of peoples undertaken at the Institute of Fine Arts of New York University.[44] From 1953, he also claims to have drawn up maps, tables and diagrams regularly on the following subjects: Russian history (1953), prehistoric Chinese art (1958), all past styles, movements, schools and artists in art history ("incomplete") (1955-60), all past styles, movements, schools and artists in art history in three dimensions (1958-66), all fields of human knowledge, intended as a "learning machine" (1969), a history of the avantgarde ("still in progress") (from 1966) and the monuments of the world ("still in progress") (from 1972).[45]

His magnum opus covering all fields of art history and entitled **Fragments of a History of Art (Time-Space) Chart** bore the subtitle **3 D system of information, presentation & storage**. All manuscript lists, excerpts, sections and their attempted transposition to a 180 x 360cm paper format (and later an integrated filing system with cards) were based, like his other diagrams and maps or the "monuments"[46] he later listed for a world culture tour, on Maciunas' compiled concepts of order. For example, in the **History of Art (Time-Space) Chart**, he pasted hand-written topographical art data together to create a synchronous and diachronous system of cross-references, which was clearly intended to ensure a complete listing of innumerable individual phenomena. It must have taken days just to copy the thirteen surviving hand-written sections.

The painstakingly composed graphic work begins around 750 B.C. and Maciunas listed under the headings "Late Geometric", "Cretan Pottery" and the names of the islands Naxos, Chios, Samos and others, the earliest known archaeological finds and evidence of daily life such as coins and ceramics from the Eastern Mediterranean area. From 700 B.C., this section on Graeco-Roman art history was supplemented by further places and an increasingly detailed distinction between styles and initial statements on individual schools. The Doric order in architecture was allocated a small, framed table with specialist terminology, beside which there was a further table with a brief description of stylistic characteristics and, further right, a third table showing early schools of Doric sculpture. In between, Maciunas had placed similar columns – mostly three or six lines 7 to 35 mm wide – listing artistic phenomena from Olympia, Sparta and Corinth. The headings and descriptions were distinguished by three different typefaces and a system of vertical and horizontal lines. From top to bottom and from right to left, Early Corinthian, Early Oriental and Oriental art were proportioned and presented in something akin to a fold-out art-historical guide, as though the purpose of the exercise had been to condense all the information from different books and travel guides into a single source, the study of which would "suffice". Graphically, the strongly vertical presentation of Greek art moved further to the right as soon as the reign of Caesar Augustus (27 B.C.–14 A.D.) heralded the emergence of "imperial art" and evidence of Christian motifs.

"Meaningful" as the entire system may have appeared to be as an impressive collection of data on world art, it is difficult to imagine any use for it beyond that. Whenever Maciunas had forgotten to include some historic phenomenon or had unwittingly accorded too much space to one particular phenomenon, a kind of erratum had to be pasted in or the entire layout had to be renewed, which meant copying it out all over again. It would seem that a large art-historical diagram spanning several continents existed after 1976.[47] However, there is no indication that the major project upon which Maciunas had embarked without a computer and on which he had continued to work for many years was anywhere near completion when he died.

In order to gain further stores of knowledge, he did not refer to certain manuals or existing charts, but consulted a large number of encyclopaedias and specialist literature. Hundreds of excerpts on a wide variety of topics have been found amongst his papers, and he deposited a considerable volume with his friend Jonas Mekas in New York in 1976.[48] On the back of a letterhead he designed himself (George Maciunas – Import Merchant, 550 Fifth Avenue, New York 36) he took notes, for example, on Early Romanesque art in Ireland and Scandinavia. The same happened with the art topography of the Spanish provinces from Asturia in the North to the Islamic-influenced areas in the South, whereby the business paper, from the period around 1959 or 1960, also bore the imprint **Books on fine arts, architecture, archaeology and history of art**.[49] From the mid 50s onwards, his main source of literature was the New York Public Library and the Library of the Metropolitan Museum of Art. Here, Maciunas not only

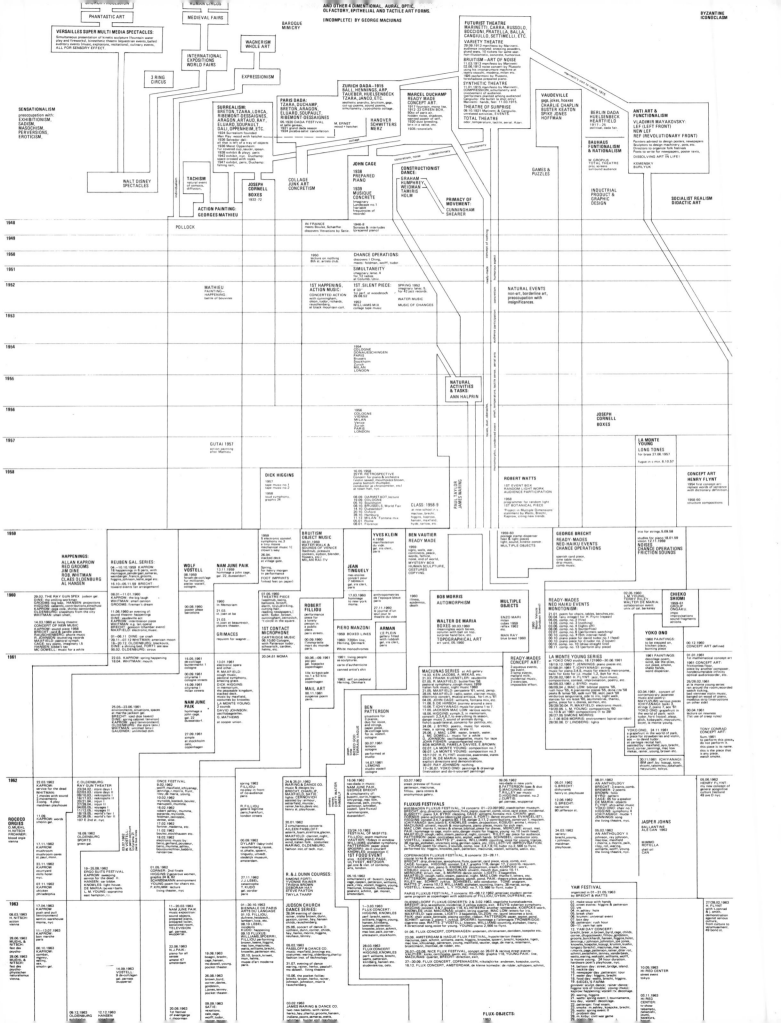

consulted topographical source material and records, but also obtained the historicising illustrations for his Fluxus magazine and for the labels of many Fluxus products.[50]

Throughout his life, he continued to study art history,[51] an undertaking in which Fluxus added an eminently practical side to his quest for a total world culture. He was well informed on virtually every country and era, and could envisage editions, concerts and even art tours in any country. He regarded the Fluxus editions of the catalogues raisonnés at the end of 1962 as an "encyclopaedia". If continued, they would result in "a nice & extensive library ... a kind of Shosoin warehouse of today," as he wrote to Robert Watts.[52] Towards the end of his life, he remarked with satisfaction that the few museums to have purchased Fluxus works invariably kept them in their libraries instead of with the other art works.[53]

In order to establish Fluxus as an art-historical concept of substance, he not only consulted encyclopaedias, but also looked into such concepts as the "simesodial cycle", studied development models such as the double helix structure, learned about distribution curves and read such books as "La Matemática de la Historia" by Alejandro Devlofev (Barcelona 1951).[54] He was constantly fascinated by character theories and by rise and fall theories. "Where is the world heading to?", "What is to become of Europe?" or "The Rhythm of History"[55] are the headings he noted. All knowledge should be systematically analysed. In the 50s, he probably read more than most art historians on Dadaism, the history of Abstract Expressionism and the European Informel as well as on contemporary Japanese art and East Asian calligraphy. He knew that not only Cage, but also Georges Mathieu, had been attracted to Zen.

He took a keen interest in abstract art for several years and names such as **Concretism** or **Fluxus** are actually products of Maciunas' reading background directed primarily against all things obscure, magical, ritual or existential and against histrionic self-referentiality in art. In contrast to painting, "abstract" writing, as in contemporary Japanese art, was not a source of suspicion, being so obviously derived from ancient artisanal crafts and customs.[56] **Concretism** emerged in one of the early excerpts on the theme of abstraction simply as a "reaction against abstract formalism".[57] He noted "laughter" as a form of human expression in which the entire body is transformed into an "apparatus of expression", whereby primitive cultures, in contrast to higher cultures, would permit more lively effects: "toto corpore" stood alongside the term "uninhibited laughter".[58]

He illustrated many excerpts with sketches, and some even with small photos. In addition to English literature, he appears to have regularly read German, French and even Slavonic texts. Around 1955, he attempted to draw up a list of artists' names and, during the years in which he studied the early mediaeval migration of peoples, he took notes on the back of specially printed delivery forms and invoices for **baroque musical instruments: harpsichords, clavichords, spinets, lutes**, listing dozens of pages of literature on Sumerian-Assyrian and

Indo-Germanic art.[59] The idea of undertaking an Eastern European and Siberian tour after performances with Fluxus artists in Germany, France, Denmark, Holland and Great Britain, was plausible not only because of his early mediaeval tribal migration studies; Maciunas had already noted all the addresses of Russian museums in 1958, and his dream of Fluxus was probably nothing less than a dream of setting out, laughing, with his colleagues, to embark upon a new tribal migration directed against the abstract formalism of the painting of the 50s, with an effect in some ways comparable to the sweeping invasion of the Huns.

Since his childhood, Maciunas himself had also undertaken a very long journey. He was born in 1931 in Kaunas, Lithuania. When he was one and a half years old, he spent several weeks in Switzerland with his little sister who was suffering from tuberculosis. Jurgis himself was dogged by bronchial ailments and ear infections from an early age and he contracted tuberculosis at the age of three. Both children were hospitalised for three months with fever in a sanatorium. While they were there, Maciunas' mother, who had occasionally performed as an opera singer and dancer before the birth of her son, played them records and danced to them.[60] Once they had recovered, she placed them in the care of a family where they grew up amongst other children aged between eight and ten. There they spent many of their convalescent hours in beds on the balcony. When Jurgis' father was first reunited with his three-year-old son, he could not understand this reportedly silent and monosyllabic child, because Jurgis spoke only French. Just six months later, the boy required further medical treatment. Each time, his mother had returned for as long as four months to Lithuania. She described how the child, who no longer wished to play with his comrades in Lithuania, always wanted to stay near her after that. The fear of losing his mother again was later to become so strong that Maciunas tried to persuade her in letters and in discussions to continue living with him. He avoided sexual relations with other women to achieve this end.[61]

At the age of eight, as his mother wrote in a twenty-page manuscript on her son, he refused to continue the piano lessons he had been taking since before he started school, because, he claimed, music was only for women. His mother also reports that Jurgis had to have his appendix removed without anaesthetic.

In 1944, the adolescent Jurgis Maciunas fled with his family before the advancing Soviet army and sought refuge in Germany, where they settled in Bad Nauheim through 1947. Once, while gathering coal along the railway tracks, he was caught unawares by an American air-raid, but not injured. His father was able to find work as an electrical engineer in the American occupied zone after the war. From 1946 onwards, Jurgis attended a Lithuanian secondary school where his talent for drawing and mathematics was noted. During this time, he built a plywood model of his parents' country house in Lithuania following the technical instructions of his father. It would appear that he read Dostoyevski's "Crime and Punishment" in English in 1947.

In 1948, the family emigrated to the USA, where they lived for several years in a middle-class housing area on Long Island. His father died there under

Collaboration of Robert Filliou, George Maciunas, Peter
Moore, Daniel Spoerri and Robert Watts (**Monsters Are
Inoffensive** [s. No. 51]) on a **table cloth** project showing
hands, noses and heads.

mysterious circumstances in 1954,[62] and the daughter married one year later. The house was then sold and Maciunas moved with his mother to 86th Street in Manhattan. He began studying art history, having previously enroled for courses in graphic design, architecture and musicology. After that he seems to have been primarily concerned about gaining a degree for his painstaking work on the world history diagram. "We both dreamed how he would become a professor and how we would travel during the long vacations," his mother wrote.[63] But the elderly professor, who had introduced her son to art history and had taken such an interest in his progress, died. Maciunas failed his exams and refused to take the foreign language tests again. Around that time, it would seem that some young Communist sympathisers entered his life and worked with Jurgis on his plans to publish a **Fluxus** magazine. As his mother relates, the Lithuanian Society, which was to have financed the magazine originally, then gave her son the cold shoulder because they felt that, in New York, they had been lucky to escape Communism in the first place. The incident prompted Jurgis to break away from his Lithuanian community and adopt the name of George.

He tried earning his living by trading in rare musical instruments, books and delicatessen foods, primarily with the aim of financing his newly opened AG Gallery on Madison Avenue. In the months from March to July 1961, when he organised concerts on historic instruments parallel to the first exhibitions and performances by the Fluxus artists under the title **Musica Antiqva et Nova**,[64] he incurred such enormous losses that he decided to take on a job with the US army in Wiesbaden as an architect in order to flee from his creditors in New York in the autumn of 1961.

In the hotel and in the apartment with his mother in Germany, he prepared the "Fluxus Internationale Festspiele Neuester Musik", a music festival which was to take place a few months later in the auditorium of the municipal museum in Wiesbaden. Although his mother knew that this extraordinary event was even to be reported on TV, she first heard of the results from her horrified neighbours. "With both feet in the grand piano" reported the *Mannheimer Morgen* on 3rd September, "Has anti-art broken out in the West?" asked *Der Mittag* on 3rd October 1962. According to his mother,

*"It was so difficult for me to see how completely absorbed he was in something so absolutely incomprehensible and strange to me."* [65]

She left her son to travel for three months to Brazil. He begged her to return and, in the months that followed, he kept each forthcoming Fluxus concert a secret from her. In this way, she experienced the journeys for Fluxus to Belgium, Holland, France, Italy and Austria until 1963 as halcyon days with her son, who showed her all the places of interests and explained them knowledgeably. Later, in New York, when they were living together again, she heard little about the Fluxus concerts and publications. When he had spent the day studying texts and designing brochures, mother and son would dedicate their evenings to the pursuit of high art, watching films, going to the theatre, visiting the mediaeval collection of The Cloisters on a Sunday, or going to the ballet. Maciunas suffered financial difficulties and, at times, ran into problems with the authorities, but, according to his mother, he would always shrug these things off, laughing about them like a child. One day, however, in connection with the debts and work carried out on a building for the **Flux Housing Cooperative**, two Italians had attacked her son in a dark doorway and had beaten him with iron bars to within an inch of his life.

After this serious incident in 1976, Maciunas made one last attempt and bought a farm in Massachusetts. Again, he ran into debt. Again, no one but his mother was willing to accompany him. The house was, of course, intended for all Fluxus artists. They were to live there, work there and perform there. However, as Maciunas had asthma, they would not be allowed to smoke anywhere on the premises. Once again, a precise set of house-rules had been drawn up before a single Fluxus artist had so much as set foot in the building. His mother was prepared to clean the thirty or so rooms, the corridors and the veranda of the dilapidated house for a time. But after one winter, she travelled to Florida for health reasons.

In the summer of 1977, Maciunas developed cancer. He knew he would not survive the following year. In February 1978, he married Billie Hutchins who had been with him for several months and who quietly admired his work. At the wedding, he and the bride exchanged clothes in a final Fluxus performance. After that, Maciunas, with whom Larry Miller had also been working closely at the time, gave a final interview. He not only referred to Dada, Cage, gags and the idea of the movement. He also saw himself, together with the other Fluxus artists, as a kind of joker. They had no real function. "I make jokes!" he had purportedly once said to a banker. "Oh, you're not going to make a joke out of the mortgage now, will you?" the banker had retorted.

The barely conceivable solitude of Maciunas' childhood, the rootlessness of having neither homeland nor history – factors which profoundly influenced his studies and later his Fluxus activities – the financial and spatial strictures which made his double life of commitment to his mother and Fluxus virtually impossible, the number of new challenges to which he constantly rose, seeking to fulfil them with military bravado, all ensured that the great vision of Fluxus world art was as in a Kafka novel postponed permanently. It was always only partly achieved. It is a vision perhaps better suited to an era when the affluent society is beginning to lose its interest in individual goods and instant satisfaction in favour of grander concepts.

Maciunas did not have a hegemony of migrant peoples in mind. All the artists who would have stopped over with him at the junctions between Madison Avenue and Siberia were to offer their superfluous artistic talent as though for the Marxist utopia of a classless society. In terms of art history, that is neither avantgarde nor postmodern. It basically says is that high art inherited from the realms of our parents can sometimes be a source of suffering.

1. This assumption appears legitimate only in the sense that Beuys scholars attribute the origins of Fluxus vaguely to John Cage and a **group** of artists, rather than to the intentions and publishing activities of George Maciunas. Reading between the lines, the aim of this assumption has always been to present Beuys' concept of Fluxus as particularly profound and "right" (an early example of this is Johannes Stüttgen, "Fluxus und der 'Erweiterte Kunstbegriff'", pp. 53-63. Published in: **Kunstmagazin**, vol.20, issue II, 1980. See also: Uwe M. Schneede **Joseph Beuys. Die Aktionen. Kommentiertes Werkverzeichnis mit fotografischen Dokumentationen.** Ostfildern-Ruit bei Stuttgart: published by Verlag Gerd Hatje, 1994, pp. 10-11) (see also notes 27 and 32).

2. This question is dealt with in depth by Hendricks 1988, pp. 21-28 and in the dissertation by Smith 1991 (see the bibliography at the end of the book, pp. 139-142).

3. Emmett Williams. "Die Leiden des jungen Emmetts", pp. 178-182; 179. Published in: **Kunstforum International** vol. 115 (September/October 1991).

4. Most recent exhibitions: **Fluxusbritannica. Aspects of the Fluxus Movement 1962-73**. London, Tate Gallery Archive Display, 29.3.-19.6.1994. **Fluxus in Deutschland 1962-1994.** Stuttgart: Institut für Auslandsbeziehungen, planned as a touring exhibition for 1995.

5. The only two comprehensive collections are the Archiv Sohm in Stuttgart and the Gilbert and Lila Silverman Fluxus Collection, Detroit and New York. The first forms part of the library collection of the Staatsgalerie Stuttgart and the second is owned privately. This "bibliophile" aspect also applies to the Fluxus collections of the Centre Georges Pompidou, Paris (initiated by Pontus Hultén, see note 53) or in the Tate Gallery, London (see note 4). A Fluxus exhibition at the Museum of Modern Art, New York, in 1988, had to be held in a tiny space in the library (exh. cat. Hendricks, Jon, and Clive Phillpot). In the German-speaking world, several private collectors – most notably Wolfgang Hahn for the Museum Moderner Kunst, Vienna, Wolfgang Feelisch and Siegfried Cremer for the Museum am Ostwall, Dortmund, and more recently René Block for the Statens Museum for Kunst, Copenhagen – have endeavoured to achieve the integration of Fluxus in museum collections. In these cases, original works by artists belonging to the Fluxus circle were generally shown, though the editions by Maciunas were rarely shown.

6. The auction of **Property from the Estate of Charlotte Moorman** on 24 June 1993 at Sotheby's, London, indicated a considerable decline, even though these were original works by Fluxus artists and not Fluxus editions. Fluxus editions are generally sold only in antiquarian book shops.

7. "We would like to have credit cards without having to pay at the end of the month. And we're going to get them. If we don't, there's going to be a catastrophe", said **John Cage** in 1967 (cited in Richard Kostelanetz. **John Cage**. Cologne: published by DuMont, 1973, pp. 38-39) referring to the futuristic visions of Richard Buckminster Fuller and Marshall McLuhan.

8. Theodor W. Adorno's posthumously published **Aesthetic Theory** and his philosophical text **Negative Dialectics** are excellent examples of this. In the field of cultural criticism, the writings of Günther Anders, particularly his concept of "apocalypse blindness" are noteworthy. The shoulder-shrugging scepticism of older Fluxus artists with regard to the "achievements" and "hazards" of the modern consumer society was probably appreciated by hardly anybody precisely because such an attitude had been denied over the decades.

9. See Marco Livingstone, ed. **The Pop Art Show**. exh. cat. London: Royal Academy of Arts, 1991.

10. Alexander Mitscherlich. "Happenings, organisierter Unfug", pp. 106-114. Published in: **Neue Rundschau.** Vol. 77, no. 1, 1966. The ineffectiveness of happenings became proverbial with Jean Tinguely's **Homage to New York** 1960 in the courtyard of the Museum of Modern Art: "This is what social protest has fallen to in our day – a garden party." Tinguely's colleague Billy Klüver then chose "The Garden Party" as the title for his official description of the event (documentation on this has been published by Pontus Hultén. **Jean Tinguely, Méta**. Berlin: published by Propyläen Verlag, 1972, p. 127 ff). A few years before the Cologne exhibition **Happenings & Fluxus** 1970 (see exh. cat. Sohm, Hanns, and Harald Szeemann), Wolf Vostell had commissioned a cutting service to collect news items on the concept of "Happening". There are several files containing these cuttings in the Archiv Sohm, Staatsgalerie Stuttgart.

11. Newspaper cuttings from 1963 onwards can be found in the Archiv Sohm, Staatsgalerie Stuttgart.

12. The term **Intermedia** was coined by Dick Higgins in February 1966 in his essay of the same name in **the something else NEWSLETTER** and was clearly intended as an alternative to the Fluxus concept. On this basis, Ina Blom submitted a dissertation to the University of Oslo in 1993 entitled **The Intermedia Dynamic. An Aspect of Fluxus** (a copy of which is held by the Archiv Sohm, Staatsgalerie Stuttgart). For a general outline of the history of Intermedia art after 1945, see my book entitled **Fröhliche Wissenschaft. Das Archiv Sohm** (Kellein 1986).

[13] "As the museum approaches the end of the century and is engaged in reassessing its functions, its aesthetic values, its very place in society, Fluxus offers a useful model for considering such issues", wrote Kathy Halbreich in her introduction to the largest Fluxus exhibition so far, held in 1993 at the Walker Art Center in Minneapolis (Armstrong, Elizabeth and Joan Rothfuss 1993, p. 11).

[14] The Fluxus documentation collected by Hanns Sohm was built up from 1963 onwards. Jean Brown collected Fluxus documents from 1972 onwards and later sold her archive to the Getty Museum. The Gilbert and Lila Silverman Fluxus Collection was started in the late 70s. In all cases, several thousand items bear witness to the subject.

[15] See note 3.

[16] I first included the "sketch" in my Fluxus essay of 1986 (Kellein 1986); since then, awareness of Fluxus has increased, partly as a result of the joint purchase of Maciunas' estate from funds of the Silverman Fluxus Collection and the Staatsgalerie Stuttgart. In 1982, Barbara Moore wrote, "The man who ran Fluxus almost single-handedly for 13 of its 16 years was also responsible for the 'Fluxus look'." (Moore 1982, p. 38). Robert Watts said, "he wanted to do everything alone – a kind of one-man home industry." (cited in **Kunstforum International**, vol. 115 [September-October 1991], p. 153). The Fluxus artists were, of course, aware of this.

[17] For documentation on this, see Hendricks I 1983, pp. 139-157. From spring 1962 onwards, Maciunas' correspondence bore the following sender's address: **G. Maciunas, FLUXUS, J.S.-Bach-Straße 6, Wiesbaden**.

[18] From 1962, a particularly suitable candidate appeared to be Robert Watts, with whom he had corresponded in detail on the aims of Fluxus right from the start (documents in Hendricks 1983 II, pp. 149-152. See also Smith 1991, vol. II, p. 358).

[19] Reprint of the manifesto **Neo Dada in Music, Theater, Poetry, Art** read in Wuppertal on 9th June 1962, e.g. in Armstrong, Elizabeth, and Joan Rothfuss 1993, pp. 156-157.

[20] William C. Seitz, ed. **The Art of Assemblage**. exh. cat. New York: Museum of Modern Art, 1961.

[21] Letter in Gilbert and Lila Silverman Fluxus Collection, New York (Inv. 01037).

[22] See Charles R. Simpson. **Soho: The Artist in the City**. Chicago and London: The University of Chicago Press, 1981, pp. 155-162.

[23] Maciunas announced **Implosions Inc. Projects** in **Fluxus Newsletter, March 8, 1967** as a joint endeavour between himself, Herman Fine and Robert Watts. See Hendricks 1988, pp. 572 and the relevant products.

[24] Letter in the Gilbert and Lila Silverman Fluxus Collection, New York (Inv. 01116). Admittedly, the sum of the hours is only 23. Similar letters were also received by other Fluxus artists (see Smith 1991, pp. 324, 346).

[25] Hendricks 1983 II, pp. 19-20.

[26] Letter in the Gilbert and Lila Silverman Fluxus Collection, New York (Inv. 01038).

[27] See catalogue no. 10, p. 34, where Beuys replaces the word "Europanism" with the word "Americanism" in the old Maciunas manifesto, signs the result and stamps it with the round stamp of "Fluxus Zone West" which includes a large cross and a smaller cross with an orb. This is the most unequivocal re-evaluation of the Fluxus idea in favour of the artist's own artistic aims.

[28] Document in Hendricks 1983 I, p. 155.

[29] Letter dated 4. April 1964 in the Archiv Sohm, Staatsgalerie Stuttgart.

[30] See no. 61, plate p. 51. With the drawing, De Maria interpreted his own wooden sculpture named "Cage", the later metal version of which is now in the Museum Moderner Kunst in Frankfurt.

[31] See Smith 1991, vol. II, p. 312.

[32] See my essay of 1986 (Kellein 1986) and my contribution "Zum Fluxus-Begriff von Joseph Beuys", pp. 137-142. In: Harlan, Volker, Dieter Koepplin and Rudolf Velhagen, eds. **Joseph Beuys-Tagung Basel 1.-4. Mai 1991 im Hardhof**, Basel: published by Wiese Verlag, 1991. In the summer of 1962, Vostell made a number of Fluxus contributions in his newly founded **décollage. Bulletin aktueller Ideen** (no. 178, p. 106). Beuys named his second exhibition at the Haus van der Grinten, Kranenburg, in 1963 "Fluxus" and, in the accompanying catalogue, he indicated that he had been active as a Fluxus artist since just after the Second World War. Both were to use the Fluxus label for many years.

[33] Letter dated 25.4.1963 in the Gilbert and Lila Silverman Fluxus Collection, New York.

[34] On 23.8.1966, Higgins wrote to Maciunas: "I have placed an inquiry with the New York State Bureau of Taxation and Finance regarding any registered exclusivity of proprietorship to the term 'Fluxus'. So far as I can tell, there is none." (Letter in the Gilbert and Lila Silverman Fluxus Collection, New York).

[35] Document in Hendricks 1983 II, pp. 164-165.

[36] Facsimile ibid., pp. 166-167.

[37] Letter in the Gilbert and Lila Silverman Fluxus Collection, New York (Inv. 01038).

[38] Letters of complaint on this subject are held by Mary Bauermeister, Cologne.

[39] Facsimile in Armstrong, Elizabeth, and Joan Rothfuss 1993, pp. 154-155.

[40] Hendricks 1983 I, p. 26.

[41] Jonas Mekas. "Notes on George Maciunas' Work in the Cinema", pp. 125-132. In **Visible Language** 26, no. 1-2 (Winter-Spring 1992).

[42] **Tulane Drama Review** 10, no. 2, Winter 1965, between pp. 100 and 101. Spike Jones, who died in 1965, was popular in the USA, particularly during the 40s, for his vaudeville programmes and cover versions of well-known music.

[43] "We opened up a store on Canal Street in, what was it, 1964, and we had it open I think almost all year. We didn't make one sale in that whole one year." (Hendricks 1983 I, p. 20).

[44] The biography was apparently compiled for the archive of Jean Brown. Many photocopies have been distributed.

[45] Existing documents on this project are either in the Gilbert and Lila Silverman Fluxus Collection, New York or in the Archiv Sohm, Staatsgalerie Stuttgart. It is no longer possible to reconstruct the individual projects, because of the lack of material. Maciunas apparently kept changing his plans.

[46] An early thirteen-page typescript **Monuments to Be Seen And Other Activities** lists a travel project from Tokyo and Kyoto through all eastern countries over a period of 101 days (original in the Gilbert and Lila Silverman Fluxus Collection, New York). According to documents in Maciunas' estate, he had obtained documents for a Fluxus round-the-world sailing tour in the mid-70s, which was planned for 1976-1984 (documents in the Archiv Sohm, Staatsgalerie Stuttgart).

[47] Information from Jon Hendricks, New York, who visited Maciunas' house several times during this period.

[48] The bulk of this is apparently in the Gilbert and Lila Silverman Fluxus Collection, New York.

[49] It is possible that this paper was not printed until 1961, when Maciunas needed money for his AG Gallery.

[50] This is evident from the signatures Maciunas noted in his excerpts. Pictorial material, especially for the **Fluxus-Newspaper**, remains to be identified.

[51] The **Calendars** of the 70s, all of which are in the Gilbert and Lila Silverman Fluxus Collection, New York, indicate that Maciunas regularly tried to continue his work on the art-historical charts.

[52] See the letter quoted in the text by Hendricks, p. 123. In March 1963, Maciunas also wanted to propose "a good library of good things being done nowaday" to Ben Vautier (postcard in the Gilbert and Lila Silverman Fluxus Collection, New York).

[53] Hendricks 1983, I, p. 27. It would therefore conform with Maciunas' wishes if Fluxus were excluded from the art world (see note 5).

[54] In the Gilbert and Lila Silverman Fluxus Collection, New York, there is a fourteen-page manuscript entitled **Historical Periodicity. For thesis only**.

[55] Ibid. The former apparently taken from Louis Emrich, undated, the latter from Edwin Francis Gay, dated 1918. For each author, he noted the periods they had adopted for a historical "cycle".

[56] Maciunas noted the names of all the calligraphic schools of the Edo period and attempted to make the connection with contemporary art in Japan on the basis of essays by, for example, Michel Seuphor in **Art d'aujourd'hui**.

[57] Document entitled **General Abstr. writing**, undated (probably late 50s) in the Gilbert and Lila Silverman Fluxus Collection, New York.

[58] On the basis of Ernst Kris, **Psychoanalytic Explorations in Art**, New York 1952, p. 225 (document also in the Silverman Collection).

[59] Documents also in the Silverman Collection.

[60] Cut-out photos and a hand-written list of their performances in the 20s were presented to the Gilbert and Lila Silverman Collection, New York, by George Maciunas' mother.

[61] The 1979 text by Maciunas' mother, entitled "My Son", a copy of which is in the Silverman Collection, New York, and the Archiv Sohm, Stuttgart, begins with the words "My son was a quiet child from birth." "I wanted him to marry very much, but he constantly said that a wife would take away a lot of valuable time from him..." (p. 10).

[62] Nam June Paik wrote: "They say, he died an unnatural death (or killed himself), c. 1952 at the youthful age of about 50. How ironic: A prominent professor in this prosperous country (USA) kills himself after having survived the Nazi invasion, the Russian invasion, and the confusion after World War II, having a talented son (architect), daughter (interior decorator), and a beautiful round-faced wife." (Ibid. in Di Maggio, Gino, and Achille Bonito Oliva 1990, pp. 246-248; 246).

[63] "My Son" (see note 61), p. 7.

[64] See frontispiece to my text and no. 67, p. 62.

[65] "My Son" (see note 61), p. 10.

[66] Hendricks 1983 I, p. 27.

## Selected Works

The artworks listed and illustrated on the following pages show much about of the nature of Fluxus:

Fluxus has neither been a style nor has it found its form through certain media. It has not been dependent one just on artist or a special group of artists, although George Maciunas, the Lithuanian designer and student of art history, has founded and shaped it since 1961.

Fluxus products range from paintings to printed matter and objects. Their sizes differ, their shapes are mostly as simple as well-known everyday objects. Many aspects of Fluxus can only be seen through photos or manifestos. Most of the works are meant to be read. This catalogue lists more than it illustrates. It contains in effect a small, concise representation of a possible Fluxus museum.

Tuesday, September 8, at 8:00 P.M.   Judson Hall (57th Street east of Seventh Avenue),

# PICKET STOCKHAUSEN CONCERT!

"jazz [Black music] is primitive... barbaric... beat and a few simple chords... garbage... [or words to that effect]" Stockhausen, Lecture, Harvard University, fall 1958

## RADICAL INTELLECTUALS:

Of all the world's cultures, aristocratic European Art has developed the most elaborate doctrine of its supremacy to all plebeian and non-European, non-white cultures. It has developed the most elaborate body of "Laws of Music" ever known: Common-Practice Harmony, 12-Tone, and all the rest, not to mention Concert etiquette. And its contempt for musics which break those Laws is limitless. Alfred Einstein, the most famous European Musicologist, said of "jazz" that it is "the most abominable treason", "decadent", and so forth. Aristocratic European Art has had a monstrous success in forcing veneration of itself on all the world, especially in the imperialist period. Everywhere that Bach, Beethoven, Bruckner and Stockhausen are hucksterd as "Music of the Masters", "Fine Music", "Music Which Will Ennoble You to Listen to It", white aristocratic European supremacy has triumphed. Its greatest success is in North America, whose rulers take the Art of West Europe's rulers as their own. There is a Brussels European Music Competition to which musicians come from all over the world; why is there no Competition, to which European Musicians come, of Arab Music? (Or Indian, or Classical Chinese, or Yoruba, or Bembey, or Tibetian percussion, or Inca, or hillbilly music?)

## STOCKHAUSEN AND HIS KIND

Stockhausen is a characteristic European-North American ruling-class Artist. His magazine, The Series, has hardly condescended to mention plebeian or non-European music at all; but when it has, as on the first page of the fourth number, it leaves no category for it except "'light music' that can be summed up by adding a question-mark after 'music' ". Stockhausen's doings are supported by the West German Government, as well as the rich Americans  J. Brimberg, J. Blinken and A. Everett. If there were a genuine equality of national cultures in the world today, if there were no discrimination against non-European cultures, Stockhausen couldn't possibly enjoy the status he does now. But Stockhausen's real importance, which separates him from the rich U.S. cretins Leonard Bernstein and Benny Goodman, is that he is a fountainhead of "ideas" to shore up the doctrine of white plutocratic European Art's supremacy, enunciated in his theoretical organ The Series and elsewhere.

## BUT THERE IS ANOTHER KIND OF INTELLECTUAL

There are other intellectuals who are restless with the domination of white plutocratic European Art. Maybe they happen to like Bo Diddley or the Everly Brothers. At any rate, they are restless with the Art maintained by the imperialist governments. To them we say: THE DOMINATION OF WHITE PLUTOCRATIC EUROPEAN ART HOLDS YOU TOO IN BONDAGE! You cannot be intellectually honest if you believe the doctrines of plutocratic European Art's supremacy, those "Laws of Art". They are arbitrary myths, maintained ultimately by the repressive violence that keeps oppressed peoples from power. Then, the domination of patrician Art-which is aristocrat-plutocrat in origin, as Opera House etiquette alone shows - condemns you to be surrounded by the stifling cultural mentality of social-climbing snobs. It binds you to the most parochial variety of the small merchant mentality, as promoted by Reader's Digest - "Music That Ennobles You to Listen to It". Even worse, though, the domination of imperialist white European plutocrat Art condemns you to live among white masses who have a sick, helpless fear of being contaminated by the "primitivism" of the colored peoples'cultures. Yes, and this sick cultural racism, not "primitive" musics, is the real barbarism. What these whites fear is actually a kind of vitality the cultures of these oppressed peoples have, which is undreamed of by their white masters. You lose this vitality. Thus, nobody who acquiesces to the domination of patrician European Art can be revolutionary culturally - no matter what else he may be.

## THE FIRST TASK

The first cultural task of radical intellectuals, especially whites, today, is:
    (1) not to produce more Art (there is too much already);
    (2) not to concede in private that non-European culture might have an "ethnic" validity;

# THE FIRST CULTURAL TASK is PUBLICLY TO EXPOSE AND FIGHT THE DOMINATION OF WHITE, EUROPEAN-U.S. RULING-CLASS ART!

Whatever path of development the non-European, non-white peoples choose for their cultures, we will fight to break out of the stifling bondage of white, plutocratic European Art's domination.

STOCKHAUSEN - PATRICIAN "THEORIST" OF WHITE SUPREMACY: GO TO HELL!

Action Against Cultural Imperialism
359 Canal Street, New York, N.Y. 10013.

(April 29, 1964: First AACI Demonstration)

1  ACTION AGAINST CULTURAL IMPERIALISM (HENRY FLYNT)

**Fight Musical Decoration of Fascism!,** April 29, 1964
Broadside, 1 page
28 x 22 cm

2  ACTION AGAINST CULTURAL IMPERIALISM (HENRY FLYNT)

**Picket Stockhausen Concert!,** September 8, 1964
Manifesto broadside designed by George Maciunas
44 x 15,5 cm

Opus 1966 is the equivalent of an infinite number of op.-66 units.
The following sub - units constitute each op.-66 unit.

| | | | | | | | |
|---|---|---|---|---|---|---|---|
| 0-1577 | THE | 0-4081 | WE | 0-8697 | MAN | | |
| 0-0164 | OF | 0-4608 | HIM | 0-4025 | ME | | |
| 0-6969 | AND | 0-0974 | BEEN | 0-8814 | EVEN | | |
| 0-5840 | TO | 0-9916 | HAS | 0-1773 | MOST | | |
| 0-8116 | A | 0-9299 | WHEN | 0-9207 | MADE | | |
| 0-6020 | IN | 0-8519 | WHO | 0-9311 | AFTER | | |
| 0-0084 | THAT | 0-0123 | WILL | 0-9345 | ALSO | | |
| 0-2284 | IS | 0-1174 | MORE | 0-1559 | DID | | |
| 0-2646 | WAS | 0-0079 | NO | 0-6853 | MANY | | |
| 0-6636 | HE | 0-4169 | IF | 0-3155 | BEFORE | | |
| 0-8666 | FOR | 0-1055 | OUT | 0-7347 | MUST | | |
| 0-1734 | IT | 0-3320 | SO | 0-1649 | THROUGH | | |
| 0-4985 | WITH | 0-4754 | SAID | 0-7969 | BACK | | |
| 0-4051 | AS | 0-1686 | WHAT | 0-8076 | YEARS | | |
| 0-4010 | HIS | 0-1116 | UP | 0-1660 | WHERE | | |
| 0-1533 | ON | 0-5934 | ITS | 0-5853 | MUCH | | |
| 0-9411 | BE | 0-7155 | ABOUT | 0-0704 | YOUR | | |
| 0-6557 | AT | 0-8403 | INTO | 0-5366 | WAY | | |
| 0-6294 | BY | 0-4817 | THAN | 0-9494 | WELL | | |
| 0-0499 | I | 0-6013 | THEM | 0-1813 | DOWN | | |
| 0-0557 | THIS | 0-3871 | CAN | 0-3131 | SHOULD | | |
| 0-2271 | HAD | 0-2391 | ONLY | 0-0536 | BECAUSE | | |
| 0-7799 | NOT | 0-8305 | OTHER | 0-4875 | EACH | | |
| 0-6812 | ARE | 0-0667 | NEW | 0-1600 | JUST | | |
| 0-1114 | BUT | 0-2677 | SOME | 0-2111 | THOSE | | |
| 0-4769 | FROM | 0-1485 | COULD | 0-4244 | PEOPLE | | |
| 0-3590 | OR | 0-4052 | TIME | 0-8446 | MR | | |
| 0-9516 | HAVE | 0-6860 | THESE | 0-8483 | HOW | | |
| 0-1745 | AN | 0-4194 | TWO | 0-2049 | TOO | | |
| 0-8029 | THEY | 0-9818 | MAY | 0-1712 | LITTLE | | |
| 0-1670 | WHICH | 0-6220 | THEN | 0-2193 | STATE | | |
| 0-4802 | ONE | 0-9403 | DO | 0-3461 | GOOD | | |
| 0-0059 | YOU | 0-7160 | FIRST | 0-1691 | VERY | | |
| 0-3393 | WERE | 0-2645 | ANY | 0-5946 | MAKE | | |
| 0-2858 | HER | 0-1792 | MY | 0-4445 | WORLD | | |
| 0-3432 | ALL | 0-6550 | NOW | 0-4925 | STILL | | |
| 0-2434 | SHE | 0-8918 | SUCH | 0-3612 | OWN | | |
| 0-0713 | THERE | 0-7442 | LIKE | 0-0725 | SEE | | |
| 0-2687 | WOULD | 0-0750 | OUR | 0-9089 | MEN | | |
| 0-4020 | THEIR | 0-1569 | OVER | 0-5525 | WORK | | |

3 ERIC ANDERSEN
**Opus,** 1966
Artist's printing with 6 scores in folded cardboard
22,5 x 15,5 cm

GEORGE MACIUNAS
Staged photograph to be used for an advertisement for the
**Fluxshop & Mail Order Warehouse**, 359 Canal Street,
New York, (Pictured from the top: Daniel Spoerri, Alison
Knowles, Dick Higgins, Ay-O, Letty Eisenhower, and George
Maciunas on sidewalk), 1964

!     !

!   .!   !

A Y O ' S

R A I N B O W

S T A I R C A S E

E N V I R O N M E N T

7 PM. TILL 10 PM

NOVEMBER 20 ONLY

$1 ENTRY CONTRIBUTION

363 CANAL ST. NEW YORK

A FLUXFEST PRESENTATION

4

4   AY-O
**Rainbow Staircase Environment,** November 20,
1964
363 Canal Street, New York
Invitation card

5   AY-O
**Flux Rain Machine,** probably late 1960's
Fluxus Edition assembled by George Maciunas
Plastic box containing moisture
3 x 12 x 9 cm

AY-O
**Portrait of Ay-O looking through a Hole,** ca. 1963
Photograph by George Maciunas

6   AY-O

**Tactile Box,** 1964
Fluxus Edition, marked A/10 D, unique version
Probably made by both George Maciunas and Ay-O
Stenciled orange cardboard box with photostatic label,
contains foam rubber
31 x 31 x 31,5 cm

7   AY-O

**The Red Landscape,** 1959
Wax and acrylic on jute
89 x 89 cm

8   AY-O

**Finger Box,** 1964
Ay-O's edition, label designed by George Maciunas for
Ay-O's exhibition at the Smolin Gallery. The box also
advertises Fluxus editions of **Finger Box** and **Tactile
Box**.
Printed paper over cardboard box containing foam
rubber
8,5 x 9,5 x 8,5 cm

6

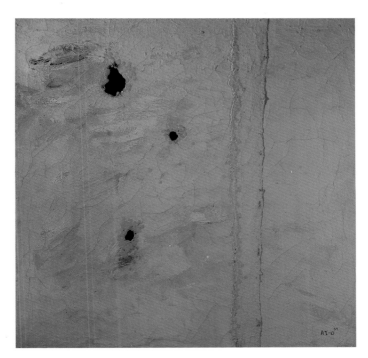

7

8

*Manifesto:*

> **2.** To affect, or bring to a certain state, by subjecting to, or treating with, a flux. "*Fluxed* into another world." *South.*
> **3.** *Med.* To cause a discharge from, as in purging.
> **flux** (flŭks), *n.* [OF., fr. L. *fluxus*, fr. *fluere, fluxum,* to flow. See FLUENT; cf. FLUSH, *n.* (of cards).] **1.** *Med.*
> **a** A flowing or fluid discharge from the bowels or other part: esp., an excessive and morbid discharge; as, the bloody *flux*, or dysentery. **b** The matter thus discharged.

*Purge* the world of bourgeois sickness, "intellectual", professional & commercialized culture, PURGE the world of dead art, imitation, artificial art, abstract art, illusionistic art, mathematical art, — PURGE THE WORLD OF "AMERICANISM"!

> **2. Act of flowing:** a continuous moving on or passing by, as of a flowing stream; a continuing succession of changes.
> **3.** A stream; copious flow; flood; outflow.
> **4.** The setting in of the tide toward the shore. Cf. REFLUX.
> **5.** State of being liquid through heat; fusion. *Rare.*

PROMOTE A REVOLUTIONARY FLOOD AND TIDE IN ART,
Promote living art, anti-art, promote NON ART REALITY to be ~~fully~~ grasped by all peoples, not only critics, dilettantes and professionals.

> **7. Chem. & Metal. a** Any substance or mixture used to promote fusion, esp. the fusion of metals or minerals. Common metallurgical fluxes are silica and silicates (acidic), lime and limestone (basic), and fluorite (neutral). **b** Any substance applied to surfaces to be joined by soldering or welding, just prior to or during the operation, to clean and free them from oxide, thus promoting their union, as rosin.

FUSE the cadres of cultural, social & political revolutionaries into united front & action.

*sonderdruck fluxus 2-3-II'63 maciunas manifest*

10

9 JOSEPH BEUYS

**Fluxus Austaellung,** October 27 - November 24, 1963
Haus van der Grinten, Kranenburg
Poster for the exhibition
84 x 64 cm

10 JOSEPH BEUYS

**Manifesto,** 1970
Alteration of George Maciunas' Fluxus Manifesto,
February 1963
From 1. Karton, Edition Hundertmark, Berlin 1970.
30 x 21 cm

11  GEORGE BRECHT

**Room,** ca. 1960
Unique, made by the artist
(**Room** was offered for sale in various early Fluxus
publications)
Silkscreen on canvas
46 x 46 cm

12  GEORGE BRECHT

**Motor Vehicle Sundown (Event),** 1960
Printed score
56 x 21,5 cm

13  GEORGE BRECHT

**Keyhole,** 1962
Framed handwritten score
Metal keyholes mounted on wooden board
Unique, made by the artist
Score: 17,2 x 14,2 x 2,2 cm
Keyhole: 12 x 9,2 x 2 cm

14  GEORGE BRECHT

**House Number,** ca. 1962
Painted wood with metal number „12"
dye stamped on front „Small Noontime House Number"
back: „For Claes"
Unique, made by the artist
(**House Number** was offered for sale in various early
Fluxus publications)
2 x 16 x 12 cm

15  GEORGE BRECHT

**White Table with Rainbow Leg,** 1962
Painted table with sun glasses and tabacco on top
Unique, made by the artist
62 x 45 x 41 cm

16  GEORGE BRECHT

**Medicine Cabinet,** 1962
Cabinet with various objects inside
Unique, made by the artist
37 x 29 x 11 cm

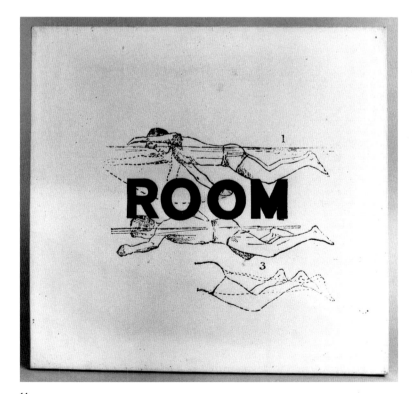

11

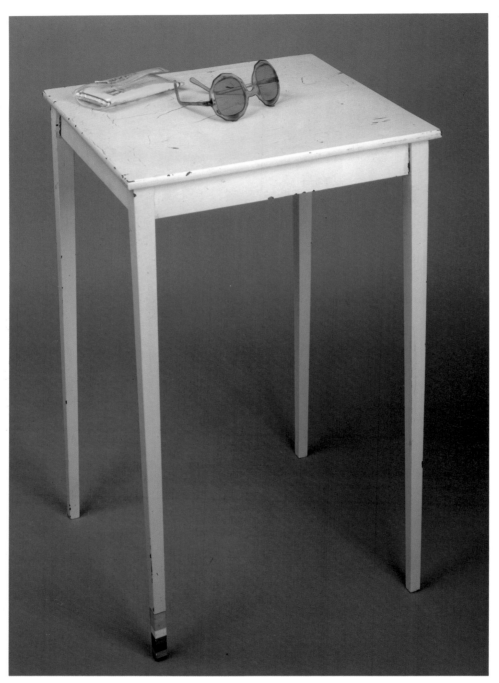

15

16

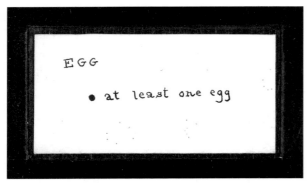

20

19

17    GEORGE BRECHT

**Start, Middle, End,** 1964, made ca. 1966
Fluxus Editions
Three flags
71,5 x 70 cm (Start)
73 x 72,5 cm (Middle)
72 x 70,5 cm (End)

18    GEORGE BRECHT

**Bolt,** ca. 1963
Barrel bolt with the word „Clock" on top, mounted on a
white painted board
Unique version, made by the artist
(**Bolts** were offered for sale through early Fluxus
publications)
86 x 9 x 16 cm

19    GEORGE BRECHT

**Exit,** ca. 1963
Red and white metal sign, unique readymade
Mounted by the artist on a white painted board
(Various versions of **Exit** were offered for sale in early
Fluxus publications)
1 x 28 x 9 cm

20    GEORGE BRECHT

**Egg – at least one egg,** January 1963
Ink on paper
Unique, made by the artist
3 x 6,5 cm

21    GEORGE BRECHT

**Five places,** January 1963
and
**Thursday,** March 1963
and
**Smoke,** March 1963
3 handwritten scores on 1 sheet of paper
Ink mounted on paper
28 x 21 cm

22    GEORGE BRECHT

**Solo for Violin,** performed May 23, 1964, by Ben
Vautier during „Fluxus Street Theatre" as a part of
„Fully Guaranteed 12 Fluxus Concerts", also called „Flux
Festival at Fluxhall", New York City
Photograph by George Maciunas, 51 x 41 cm

22

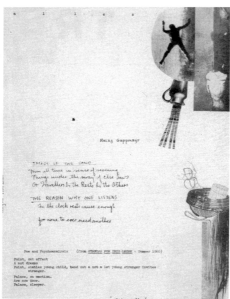

23

23 GEORGE BRECHT, Editor

**VTRE,** 1963
Metuchen, N.J., published by the artist and later
distributed by Fluxus
1 leaf, printed both sides
32 x 25 cm

24 GEORGE BRECHT, ALISON KNOWLES and
ROBERT WATTS

**Blink,** 1963
Made by the artists
Silkscreen and stencil on canvas
46 x 46 cm

25 GEORGE BRECHT and ROBERT WATTS
Collage for side 1 of
**Yam Festival Newspaper (E News Pa Pay Per),**
1963
Unique, made by the artists
74 x 15,3 cm

26 GEORGE BRECHT and ROBERT WATTS
Collage for side 2 of
**Yam Festival Newspaper (E News Pa Pay Per),**
1963
Unique, made by the artists
74 x 15,3 cm

24

27–29

27 GEORGE BRECHT

**Water Yam,** 1963
Fluxus Edition (earliest Fluxus printing) assembled by
George Maciunas
Cardboard box containing 54 scores printed black on
orange
cardstock, and 19 printed black on white cardstock
(total 73)
15 x 16,5 x 4,5 cm

28 GEORGE BRECHT

**Water Yam,** 1963
Fluxus Edition
Fiberboard box containing 65 scores printed black on
white cardstock
5 x 22,5 x 24,5 cm

29 GEORGE BRECHT

**Water Yam,** 1963/65
Fluxus Edition
Plastic box, top transparent, base black, containing
99 scores printed black on white cardstock, also contains
**Cloud Scissors** (6 cards in envelope), **Nut Bone**
(1 booklet)
13 x 18 x 3 cm

30  GEORGE BRECHT

**Games & Puzzles: Ball Puzzle/Bead Puzzle,**
n.d. (ca. 1963)
Unique prototype, made by either George Brecht or
George Maciunas for the Fluxus Edition
Wooden box containing 2 typewritten scores, 2 pieces of
ivory and 2 marbles
8 x 12 x 11 cm

31  GEORGE BRECHT

**Games & Puzzles: Inclined Plane Puzzle,** 1965
Fluxus Edition, assembled by George Maciunas
Wooden box with ball, label and score
3,5 x 9 x 27,5 cm

32  GEORGE BRECHT

**Games & Puzzles: Inclined Plane, Swim, Black
Ball Puzzle,** 1965/69
Fluxus Edition, assembled by George Maciunas
Plastic box containing 3 scores and ball
12 x 9 x 3 cm

33  GEORGE BRECHT

**Games & Puzzles: Name Kit, spell your name,**
1965/69
Fluxus Edition, assembled by George Maciunas
Plastic box containing score and various objects
3 x 9 x 12 cm

34  GEORGE BRECHT

**Games & Puzzles: Swim Puzzle,** 1965/69
Fluxus Edition, assembled by George Maciunas
Plastic box containing score and seashell
2 x 9 x 12 cm

35  GEORGE BRECHT

**Games & Puzzles: Bread Puzzle,** 1965/69
Fluxus Edition, assembled by George Maciunas
Plastic box containing score and ball
3 x 9 x 12 cm

36  GEORGE BRECHT

**Games & Puzzles: Black Ball Puzzle,** 1965/69
Fluxus Edition, assembled by George Maciunas
Plastic box containing score and 4 balls
3 x 9 x 12 cm

37  GEORGE BRECHT

**Deck, a Fluxgame,** 1966/69
Fluxus Edition
Plastic box with 64 printed playing cards
2,5 x 7 x 9,5 cm

38  GEORGE BRECHT

**(Brooklyn) Joe Jones,** 1967
Copy of a typewritten page, unique
27 x 21 cm

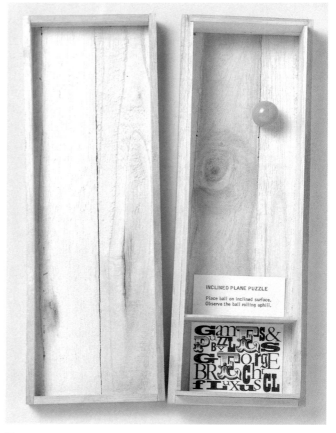

31

39 (GEORGE BRECHT/ROBERT FILLIOU)
La Cedille qui sourit

**Banqueroute,** 1968
La Cedille qui Sourit, Villefranche-s-Mer
Poster, signed
50 x 32 cm

40 GEORGE BRECHT

**Closed on Mondays, a Fluxgame,** 1969
Fluxus Edition, assembled by George Maciunas
Plastic box, black, both sides glued together
2 x 12 x 9 cm

41 GEORGE BRECHT

**Cloud Scissors** (to Robert Filliou), 1964
Envelope with 7 text pieces printed on cards
9,5 x 11,5 cm

42 GEORGE BRECHT

**A Question or more,** proposed ca. 1967, ca. 1969-70
Based on a 1959 work
Prototype by George Maciunas for a Fluxus Edition
4 components: 3 plastic boxes containing painted and
natural wood pieces from a „Scrabble" game
each 3,5 x 6,8 x 6,8 cm
and an empty space

43 GEORGE BRECHT

**Universal machine II,** 1976
Fluxus Edition, assembled by George Maciunas,
copy No. 3
Wooden box with printed instructions and illustrated
sheet, plexiglass, and a variety of organic and inorganic
objects
appr. 28 x 28 x 9 cm (not including hinges and clasp)

44 GEORGE BRECHT

**Universal Machine III**
and

GEORGE BRECHT

**Valoche/a Flux Travel Aid,** 1976
Mechanical by George Maciunas for the labels for the
Fluxus Edition
also

ROBERT FILLIOU

**Telepathic Music**
Mechanical by George Maciunas for the instructions for
the Filliou work
28 x 22 cm

45 GEORGE BRECHT

**Valoche/a flux travel aid,** 1970/1978
(Proposed versions were offerd by Fluxus starting in
1964)
Fluxus Edition, assembled by George Maciunas
Antique wood box containing a variety of childrens toys
and mysterious objects
17 x 28 x 14 cm (including a 2,8 cm lid,
excluding hinges and handle)

47

46  PHILIP CORNER

**Keyboard Dances,** ca. 1963
Unique handmade cardboard box containing 85 scores
handwritten by the artist, 2 photostated scores, 6 pages
of handwritten notes and instructions on 3 sheets of
paper. All the scores are rolled into scrolls
Box appr. 6 x 20 x 14 cm

47  ROBERT FILLIOU

**Poi Poi,** 1961
Handmade catalog with stamping-ink fingerprints,
cigarette-ends, rubber bands etc., plus two beer bottles
(one full, one empty) with positive and negative label
each 23,5 x 6 cm

48  ROBERT FILLIOU
**General Semantics A-Z,** 1967
Unique, made by the artist for Dick Higgins as the
American version of his „Sémantique Générale" of 1962
Wood, plastic letters, feltpen and paper stick pictures
147 x 183 cm

49  ROBERT FILLIOU
**The Obvious Deck,** 1967
Prototype by George Maciunas for the Fluxus Edition,
unique
Plastic box containing montage card using 2 photostats
mounted on cardstock, embellished with paint and ink
appr. 1 x 12 x 9 cm

50  ROBERT FILLIOU
**The Key to Art,** 1967
Flyer designed by George Maciunas announcing
photographs of 5 artist's hands at Tiffany's, New York,
and 2 Fluxus Editions of a 24 hour hand clock and hand
prints
42 x 20 cm

51  ROBERT FILLIOU/DANIEL SPOERRI AND
ROLAND TOPOR
**Monsters Are Inoffensive,** copyrighted in 1967,
produced in 1968
22 different printed cards in plastic box
Fluxus Edition
1,5 x 18 x 13 cm

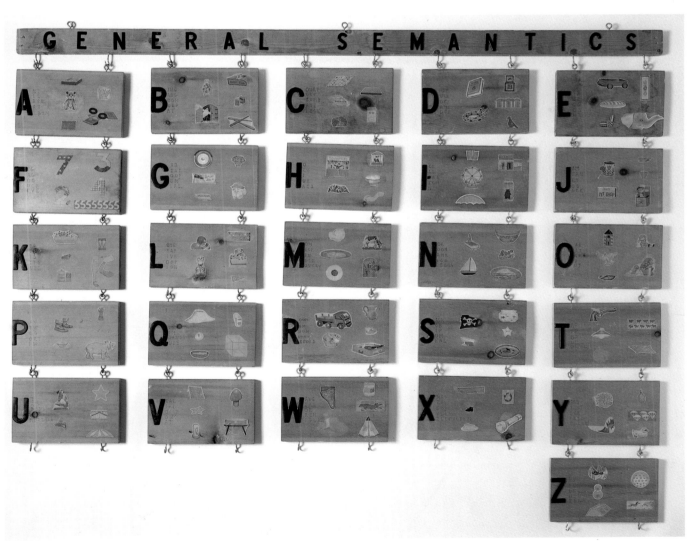

48

## 52 ROBERT FILLIOU

**De la galerie Légitime,** January 1962
Mimeographed typewritten page, unsigned
29,5 x 21 cm

53

## 53 ROBERT FILLIOU

**Galerie Légitime,** ca. 1962-63
Made by the artist
Assemblage
Hat with rubber stamped initialled cloth label on the
inside. Handmade rubber stamped manilla box,
handmade rubber stamped orange paper box with
typewritten score, and 2 small coins, a rubber stamped
coupage of a number of leaves of a journal stapled and
cut into the shape of a face
4 x 26,5 x 26,5 cm

DE LA GALE IE LÉGITIME

J'ai créé la Galerie Légitime
en Janvier 1962.

La toute première Galerie fut ma
première casquette, achetée 10 ans
auparavant à Tokio. Les oeuvres
exposées le long des rues de Paris
étaient ma création.

Plus tard, en Allemagne où se pour-
suivait le voyage, on me vola ma
Galerie. Est-ce par esprit de com-
pensation que la Télévision allemande
vint un mois plus tard rue des Rosiers
filmer les pérégrinations de la nouvel-
le Galerie (une autre casquette).

En Juillet 1962, la Galerie Légitime
— un chapeau en l'occurence — organi-
sa une exposition des oeuvres de l'artiste américain Benjamin Patterson.
Nous parcourûmes Paris de 4 heures du
matin à 21 heures — départ des Halles,
arrivée à la Coupole.

En Octobre 1962, à Londres, la Galerie
Légitime — un chapeau melon, bien sûr
— exposa au cours de la Misfits' Fair
des oeuvres de Vautier, Williams, Page,
Kopcke, Spoerri, Filliou. C'était
"l'exposition congelée" dont le vernis-
sage avait lieu du 22 Octobre 1962 au
22 Octobre 1972. A cet effet la Galerie
était placée dans un sac frigorifique,
et y restera jusqu'à la dâte prévue.

Voici donc à présent les branches
autonomes. Il est fortement conseil-
lé au propriétaire de chacune de s'en
coiffer de temps en temps: dans les
rues, au cours de soirées, vernissages,
etc..., car son aspect poésie vivante,
d'action, de comportement n'est point
négligeable.

De là provient d'ailleurs son nom.
Car je considérais légitime que l'art
descende, de ses hauteurs, dans la rue.
Et aussi, vu le destin catastrophique
de l'artiste dans une société qui l'ac-
cule à la misère ou à la prostitution,
que tout ce qu'il pouvait bien (ou mal)
faire pour gagner de l'argent était légitime.

Aïe! Aïe! Aïe!

55/56

57

**4** GEORGE MACIUNAS

**Fluxus Preview Review,** 1963
Published by Fluxus, Köln-Mülheim, West Germany
Printed paper roll
167 x 10 cm

**5** **Fluxus 1,** Proposed 1961-62, realized Winter 1964-65
Fluxus Edition, assembled and edited by George
Maciunas
Wooden box with burned in title. The contents of
manilla envelopes and translucent sheets are bolted
together and contain printed scores, a variety of
readymade and constructed objects, printed photographs,
etc. Contains works by: Ay-O, George Brecht, Stanley
Brouwn, Guiseppe Chiari, Congo, Robert Filliou, Brion
Gysin, Sohei Hashimoto, Dick Higgins, Joe Jones, Alison
Knowles, Takehisa Kosugi, Shigeko Kubota, György
Ligeti, George Maciunas, Jackson Mac Low, Benjamin
Patterson, Takako Saito, Tomas Schmit, Mieko (Chieko)
Shiomi, Ben Vautier, Robert Watts, Emmett Williams,
La Monte Young
5 x 22,5 x 24,3 cm

**6** **Fluxus 1** (without box), 1964
Fluxus Edition, assembled and edited by George
Maciunas
Book with envelopes bolted together, containing works
by George Brecht, Dick Higgins, Joe Jones, Takehisa
Kosugi, György Ligeti, George Maciunas, Jackson Mac
Low, Benjamin Patterson, Ben Vautier, Emmett
Williams and La Monte Young
3,5 x 21 x 19 cm

**7** **Flux Year Box 2** ('A' copy), proposed 1965,
realized ca. 1968
Fluxus Edition, assembled by George Maciunas
Silkscreened wood box with interior partitions
containing works by George Brecht, Shigeko Kubota,
Ken Friedman, Ben Vautier, Claes Oldenburg, Jim
Riddle, Fred Lieberman, Robert Watts, Albert Fine,
Benjamin Patterson, Paul Sharits, Willem DeRidder, and
Bob Scheff. Contains 6 program cards for
**Fluxorchestra at Carnegie Recital Hall,** a film
viewer, film loops by: Eric Andersen, John Cale, George
Brecht, John Cavanaugh, Herman Fine, Dan Laufer,
George Maciunas, Yoko Ono, Paul Sharits, Stanley van
der Beek, Robert Watts, Wolf Vostell. This work also
contains namecards of the artists included.
9 x 20 x 20 cm

54

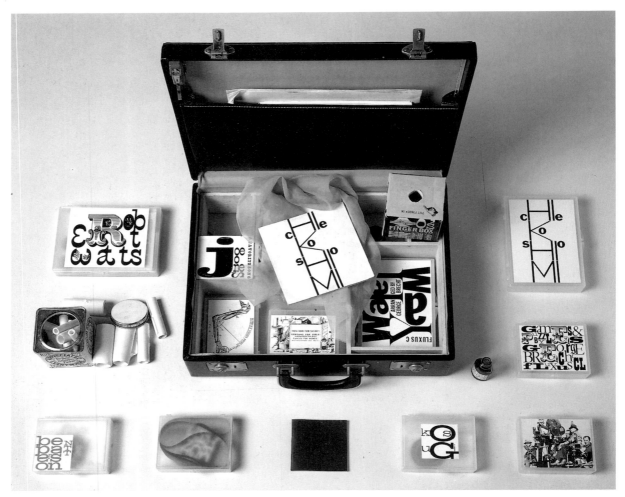

59

58 **Fluxkit** ('A' copy), 1964
Fluxus Edition, unique copy assembled by George
Maciunas
Stenciled businessmen's attaché case with interior wood
partitions/compartments containing **Fluxus
Newspapers** Nos. 1, 2 and 3, George Brecht's
Newspaper, Fluxus Editions assembled by Mieko
Shiomi, Joe Jones, and Benjamin Patterson, and Fluxus
Editions, including some unique prototypes assembled
by George Maciunas of works by Ben Vautier, Alison
Knowles, Robert Watts, Takehisa Kosugi, Dick Higgins,
Nam June Paik, George Brecht, Ay-O, La Monte
Young, and Emmett Williams
12,5 x 43 x 32 cm

59 **Fluxkit,** after 1964
Fluxus Edition assembled by George Maciunas,
including works made by Ay-O, Brecht, Higgins, Jones,
Knowles, Kosugi, Maciunas, Patterson, Paik, Shiomi,
Watts as well as collective Fluxus Editions
12 x 43 x 33 cm

60 **Flux Paper Games: Rolls and Folds,** proposed 1966,
realized ca. 1969
Fluxus Edition, deluxe version, assembled by George
Maciunas, using elements made by Bob Grimes, Greg
Sharits, Paul Sharits and David Thompson
Wood box containing printed material, marbles, film,
gun powder, matches etc.
30,5 x 30,5 x 4,8 cm

FLUXUS NEWSPAPER (Nos. 61 - 66)

61 **Fluxus cc V TRE Fluxus
(Fluxus Newspaper No. 1),**
January 1964
Edited by George Brecht and Fluxus Editorial Council,
New York
Fluxus Edition
58,5 x 46 cm, 4 pages

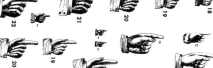

CTION

e to observe a sign
ting direction of travel.

- travel in the indicated direction
- travel in another direction

One Hundred

one one one one one one one one one

one one one one one one one one

one one one one one one one

one one one one one one one one

one one one one one one one

one one one one one one one one

one one one one one one one one

*the
"n"
ber*

Jackson Mac Low
15 December 1961
965 Hoe Avenue
New York 59 N Y

# LINCOLN CENTER
*for The Performing Arts*

ILHARMONIC TAKES ON THE AVANT-GARDE

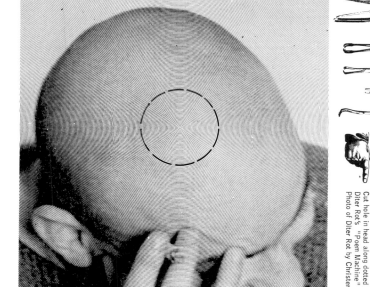

Cut hole in head along dotted line to produce
Diter Rot's "Poem Machine"
Photo of Diter Rot by Christer Christian

SAFETY
STARTS
BETWEEN
THE
EARS

: from a richard maxfield concert :

elektrahnik nachtmusick

I (for j. mac 1.)
thiqu thas toss bambu jungel
redlaqu doors open ope pian o
whips whisperattl whisqueak
flah flashappen whippoowont
grasshapper hoppenin wirrt

fistfog mogfist grassqueak
no nolow leanda meanda meout
molloi symph sypath seasymph
tymph tatymph tatame ti ti
meta metaph mustaf a firsfog

jim himweed jimweed jinjoynt
joyjoynt joboy jobi jajaw jajo
jaqu kennabekkon bak bak
gaimin gamindragon dragonese

o dragonfligh courss down o
trem thik bamboo juggl o citie
thinroad owt spewspowt a yew

II (for r. e. b.)
a luv lettus be kine to 1
anuth mi crien pine wheel o
disextabl rive und than nie
zi glori un into undate arrs
nubil skit lightn in cri
crak has haus dor un woodwatch
skïi skut ut opcit ut nemsu
kung dovid mof un majestum
thet u shud be l hoo underst
thet war approche thet armi
muve down olda mudded rode
ainsaqua is own foetus shee
muven in shellaform w/ alla
shelles fallin aroun sich
und marrow twang et sprachen
sprung out finlmente massa ze
zuider cumen seed mein ovari
okapi disguys sthil burnt fr
yest ope kati katzen katsumi
unden orientar skimme schiml
aber ober ajeck abjeck i kamen
thu awry tu u wear wadin wid
luk lak masse mi qui veut yu

III (for r. k.)
nacht au sich eine cleensmel
hartcriket dikkn ownin cocoon
neetwon ya yup up owen jorge
ye mudfox joice fuxratholy em
twen um nicht nacht blossum
fratwind movin eyah in er eye
ah seez ye hrtbeest makkin a
maxum stima to trema chees
breadrats turnum out each cam
camholy ovah rest inta robot
summa robot frossbottumd cole
ingermain letme lakme blud em
spel vykewishe vosc vobis bosk

IV (for d. w.)
winda somun awakenin on my
grayv gravitie it moonshammy
la monatque turnov brïd beerd
gi rabel gi semin ol vulner ol
shi corason aguilah wast zim
watta bufalch falla outa fr to
nowland thatrain humz atque
thistren go grounmisst ga pine
doun hollough upp mts tis ov
thei halu mi countrie uv wind uv
wiv sighlant weve upin nachtwind

carol bergé
new york city
april 1961

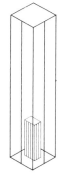

Portrait of John Cage

Portrait of the School
of Cage, Caged
(De Maria 62)

. Feldman                    by permission from PUNCH

I HEAR
A NOISE
DOWNSTAIRS

WHY WORRY? LET "FREDDIE" DO IT
Meet "Fretful Freddie"...the original worry bird. One look at his
doleful face—and you'll know he
can do a better job than you. Keep
him handy—and remember: "Don't
be sad, don't be blue; 'Cause I'm
the bird who'll worry for you."
No. 173—"Fretful Freddie" . . . $1.49

HELLO? HELLO!
THIS YOU, CHARLEY?
WHAT? WHO IS THIS?
I WANT T'TALK TO
CHARLEY!

May Green

"Et quand vous nous dites que
OVIÉTIQUE PATRIE,
est not PLUS JUSTE RIE,
S L'HISTOIRE DE L.ard. Nous
ous les . . ers."

DIAL
LIBERTÉ

Décollage by Raymond Hains and Jacques de la Villegle, 1950

NE OF THE BEST!"
—DAILY NEWS

"IMPRESSIVE!"
—JOURNAL AMERICAN

EMORABLE!"
—WORLD TELEGRAM

"A GIGANTIC DRAMA!"
—CUE MAGAZINE

N EPIC!"
—TIME MAGAZINE

"BRILLIANT!"
—HERALD TRIBUNE

"A TRIUMPH!"
—NEWSDAY

62 **Fluxus cc V TRE Fluxus (Fluxus Newspaper No. 2),**
February 1964
Edited by George Brecht and Fluxus Editorial Council,
New York
Fluxus Edition
57 x 44,5 cm, 4 pages

63 **Fluxus cc fiVe ThReE (Fluxus Newspaper No. 4),**
June 1964
Edited by Fluxus Editorial Council, New York
Fluxus Edition
58 x 46 cm, 4 pages

64 **Fluxus Vaseline sTREet
(Fluxus Newspaper No. 8),**
May 1966
Edited by George Maciunas, New York
Fluxus Edition
55,5 x 43 cm, 4 pages

65 Mechanical for page 4 of **Fluxus Vaseline sTREet
(Fluxus Newspaper No. 8),** ca. Spring 1966
Designed by George Maciunas
Mechanical for the Fluxus Edition consisting of pasted
blocks of type, halftones, and handdrawn guidelines
66,5 x 47 cm

66 **V TRE (Fluxus Magazine),** New York, 1964-1970
No. 1 - 9
Designed and edited by George Maciunas
Facsimile reprint by Giancarlo Politi, Flash Art,
Milano 1972

POSTERS, PROGRAMS AND
PRINTED ANNOUNCEMENTS
RELATED TO FLUXUS (Nos. 67 - 112)

67 **Musica Antiqva et Nova,** 1961
Programs for concerts at AG Gallery, 925 Madison Ave,
New York
Designed by George Maciunas
– March 25 to May 14, 1961
– May 7 to May 28, 1961
– June 4 to June 25, 1961
– June 10 to June 24, 1961
– July 9 to July 30, 1961
Various sizes, appr. 9 x 35 cm

68 **Neo-Dada in der Musik,** Kammerspiele Düsseldorf,
June 16, 1962
Concert program with publication-prospect
19,5 x 42,5 cm

69 **Fluxus Internationale Festspiele Neuester Musik,**
September 1-23, 1962
Hörsaal des Städtischen Museums, Wiesbaden
Poster program designed by George Maciunas
(black on white)
42 x 30 cm

70 **Fluxus Internationale Festspiele Neuester Musik,**
September 1-23, 1962
Hörsaal des Städtischen Museums, Wiesbaden
Poster program designed by George Maciunas
(black on orange)
28 x 20 cm

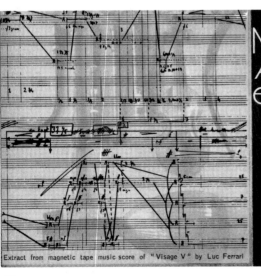

67

# FLUXUS *INTERNATIONALE FESTSPIELE
# NEUESTER MUSIK

## IM HÖRSAAL DES STÄDTISCHEN MUSEUMS, WIESBADEN

**AMSTAG . EPT. 962 4:30 UHR** KONZERT NR.1, KLAVIER KOMPOSITIONEN - U.S.A., K.E.WELIN UND F.RZEWSKI - PIANISTEN. JOHN CAGE: 31'57.9864"/PHILIP CORNER: KLAVIER TATIGKEITEN (FÜR EIN KLAVIER UND VIELE SPIELER) & FLUX & FORM NR. 7 & 14 / TERRY RILEY: KONZERT FÜR 2 PIANISTEN UND TONBAND / T.JENNINGS: KLAVIER STÜCKE / JED CURTIS: KLAVIER STÜCK / GRIFITH ROSE: 2. ENNEAD / DICK HIGGINS: CONSTELLATION NR.1(FÜR 2 KLAVIERE UND 3 RADIOS) / LA MONTE YOUNG: "566" FÜR HENRY FLYNT & KLAVIER STÜCKE FÜR DAVID TUDOR NR.2 / GEORGE BRECHT: FÜNF KLAVIER STÜCKE 1961   UND   DREI KLAVIER STÜCKE 1962

**AMSTAG . EPT. 0:00 UHR** KONZERT NR.2 KLAVIER KOMPOSITIONEN - JAPAN, K.E.WELIN - PIANIST. TOSHI ICHIYANAGI:   MUSIK FÜR KLAVIER   NR.1 BIS NR.7 / YORIAKI MATSUDAIRA: INSTRUKTIONEN FÜR KLAVIER / SHINICHI MATSUSHITA: MOSAIKEN / YOKO ONO:   EIN STÜCK UM DEN HIMMEL ZU SEHEN / KEIJIRO SATO: CALIGRAPHY / YUJI TAKAHASHI: EKSTASIS / TORU TAKEMITSU:KLAVIER ENTFERNUNG UND ÜBERGANG / YASUNAO TONE: KLAVIER TON MIT TONBAND /   GEORGE YNASA: PROJECTION ESEMPLASTIC   I, II UND III

**ONNTAG . EPT. 4:30 UHR** KONZERT NR.3, KLAVIER KOMPOSITIONEN - EUROPA, K.E.WELIN - PIANIST. K.H.STOCKHAUSEN: KLAVIERSTÜCK IV / G.LIGETI: TROIS BAGATELLES / G.M.KOENIG: 2 KLAVIER STÜCKE / KONRAD BOEHMER: KLANGSTÜCK & POTENTIAL /   JAN MORTHENSON: COURANTE / LARS J.WERLE: GRILLER FÜR PIANIST / MICHAEL VON BIEL: EIN BUCH FÜR DREI / DIETER SCHNEBEL: REACTIONS (KONZERT FÜR EINEN INSTRUMENTALISTEN & PUBLIKUM) & VISIBLE  MUSIK FÜR 1 DIRIGENTEN UND 1 INSTRUMENTALISTEN.

**ONNTAG . EPT. 0:00 UHR** KONZERT NR.4, KLAVIER KOMPOSITIONEN - EUROPA, F.RZEWSKI - PIANIST.   JACQUES CALONNE: QUADRANGLES SUIVIS DE FENETRES ET BOUCLES / PAOLO EMILIO CARAPEZZA: 9o' CIELO / GIUSEPPE CHIARI: GESTI SUL PIANO / SYLVANO BUSSOTTI: POUR CLAVIER, 5 KLAVIER STÜCKE FÜR DAVID TUDOR & PER TRE (FÜR EIN KLAVIER UND 3 PIANISTEN)/FREDERIC RZEWSKI STUDIEN & TRÄUME /   LUCIER: ACTION MUSIC FOR PIANO BOOK I /   MACCHI: TITONE /   MARCHETTI   MUSIK

**AMSTAG EPT. 0:00 UHR** KONZERT NR.5, KOMPOSITIONEN FÜR ANDERE INSTRUMENTE UND STIMMEN - U.S.A.,   GEORGE BRECHT: KARTENSTÜCK   FÜR STIMMEN / JOHN CAGE: SOLO FÜR STIMME (2) 1960 / PHILIP CORNER: PASSIONATE EXPANSE OF THE LAW /   DICK HIGGINS: CONSTELLATION NR.4 & NR.7 / TERRY JENNINGS: STREICHQUARTETT / PHILIP KRUMM:  MUSTER (FÜR STREICHQUARTETT) / JACKSON MAC LOW: BUCHSTABEN FÜR IRIS NUMMERN FÜR DIE STILLE UND   DANKE - EINE ZUSAMMENARBEIT FÜR LEUTE / TERRY RILEY: UMSCHLAG 1960 (FÜR STREICHQUARTETT) / EMMETT WILLIAMS:EIN ZWEIFELHAFTES LIED IN VIER RICHTUNGEN FÜR 5 STIMMEN / GEORGE BRECHT: STREICHQUARTETT / LA MONTE YOUNG: KOMPOSITION 1960 NR.7 (FÜR STREICHQUARTETT)

**ONNTAG . SEPT. 4:30 UHR** KONZERT NR.6, KOMPOSITIONEN FÜR ANDERE INSTRUMENTE UND STIMMEN - JAPAN, TOSHI ICHIYANAGI: STANZEN & PILE / KENJIRO EZAKI: BEWEGLICHE PULSE & DISCRETION / YORITSUNE MATSUDAIRA: EIN STÜCK FÜR SOLO FLÖTE /   YASUNAO TONE: ANAGRAMM FÜR STREICHE /   YOKO ONO:  DER PULS /

**ONNTAG . SEPT. 0:00 UHR** KONZERT NR.7, KOMPOSITIONEN FÜR ANDERE INSTRUMENTE UND STIMMEN - EUROPA, MICHAEL VON BIEL: STREICH MUSIK / GEORGE MACIUNAS: SOLO FÜR STIMME UND MIKROPHON / GRIFITH ROSE: STREICHQUARTETT / FREDERIC RZEWSKI: SOLILOQUY (FÜR VIOLINE) UND  THREE RHAPSODIES FOR SLIDE WHISTLES   / BENJAMIN PATTERSON: VARIATIONEN FÜR KONTRABASS /

**REITAG 4. EPT. 0:00 UHR** KONZERT NR.8, KONKRETE  MUSIK & HAPPENINGS - U.S.A., JOSEPH BYRD: ZWEI STÜCKE FÜR RICHARD MAXFIELD, 1960 / JOHN CAGE: VARIATIONS / GEORGE BRECHT: KARTENSTÜCK FÜR OBJEKTE,TRÖPFELNDE MUSIK ,KERZEN STÜCK FÜR RADIOS & SOLO FÜR EINEN BLÄSER / JED CURTIS: GAVOTTE, ALLEMAND, UND GIGUE / DICK HIGGINS: GEFÄHRLICHE MUSIK NR.2 UND   GRAPHIS 82 /   JACKSON MAC LOW: EIN STÜCK FÜR SARI DIENES /  TERRY RILEY: OHR STÜCK (FÜR PUBLIKUM) /

**AMSTAG 5. SEPT. 0:00 UHR** KONZERT NR.9, KONKRETE  MUSIK & HAPPENINGS - JAPAN, TOSHI ICHIYANAGI: MUSIK FÜR ELEKRISCHE METRONOM  &  IBM MUSIK / K. AKIYAMA: EINE GEHEIM METHODE / TAKENHISA KOSUGI: MICRO I & MANODHARMA I /   YOKO ONO: ZWEI STÜCKE / YASUNAO TONE: TAGE, NUMMER & UNTERREDUNG / GEORGE YNASA: MUSIQUE CONCRETE  UND   AOINOUE /

**ONNTAG 6. EPT. 0:00 UHR** KONZERT NR.10, KONKRETE  MUSIK & HAPPENINGS - INTERNATIONAL, NAM JUNE PAIK: SIMPLE /  PIERRE MERCURE: STRUC-TURES METALLIQUES NR.3 / NAM JUNE PAIK: HOMMÂGE À JOHN CAGE / ETUDE FOR PIANOFORTE   UND   SONATA QUAZI UNA FANTASIA / DIETER SCHNEBEL:SICHTBARE MUSIK FÜR EINEN DIRIGENTEN / MACIUNAS: IN MEMORIAM FÜR ADRIANO OLIVETTI / BENJAMIN PATTERSON: SEPTET AUS "LEMONS"   UND   OVERTURE (2. DARSTELLUNG)   / GEORGE BRECHT: WORD EVENT

**2. SEPT. 4:30 UHR** KONZERT NR.11, TONBAND MUSIK UND FILME  - U.S.A., JOHN CAGE: FONTANA MIX,  MUSIC FOR  THE MARRYING MAIDEN / LA MONTE YOUNG: ZWEI TÖNE  / STAN VANDERBEEK: FILMEN / DICK HIGGINS: REQUIEM  FOR WAGNER  THE CRIMINAL MAYOR

**2. SEPT. 0:00 UHR** KONZERT NR.12, TONBAND MUSIK - U.S.A.,  RICHARD MAXFIELD:   HUFTEN MUSIK /  RADIO MUSIK / DAMPF /   PASTORAL SYMPHONY / PERSPECTIVES / NACHT MUSIK

**ONNTAG 3. EPT. 4:30 UHR** KONZERT NR.13, TONBAND MUSIK UND FILME  - JAPAN, KANADA. TOSHI ICHIYANAGI: KAIKI /   NOBUTAKA MIZUNO: TONBAND STÜCK / TORU TAKEMITSU: VOCALISM A-I & WASSER MUSIK / YASUNAO TONE: COSTUME   UND  WARANIN / GEORGE YNASA: AOI-NO-UE /TESHIGAHARA: FILM / YOJI KURI: HUMAN ZOO / OSHIMA: FILM/ HANI: FILM /   ISTVAN ANHALT: COMPOSITION NR.4 /CIONI CARPI & L. PORTUGAIS: POINT ET CONTREPOINT (FILM) / MAURICE BLACKBURN: JE (FILM) /

**ONNTAG 3. EPT. 0:00 UHR** KONZERT NR.14, TONBAND MUSIK - FRANKREICH, "LES PREMIERES DECOUVERTES": P.SCHAEFFER: ETUDE AUX CASSEROL P.HENRY: MUSIQUE SANS TITRE / P.ARTHUYS: NATURE MORTE À LA GUITARE / A.HODEIR: JAZZ ET JAZZ /   "RECHERCHES RECENTES": L.FERRARI: ETUDE AUX ACCIDENTS & TÊTE ET QUEUE DU DRAGON /   F.B. MACHE:  PRÉLUDE / E. CANTON: ETUDE / J. HIDALGO: ETUDE /  B. PARMEGIANI: ETUDE /  F. BAYLE: TREMPLINS & LIGNES ET POINTS / M. PHILIPPOT: AMBIANCE II / P. CARSON: ETUDE / P. SCHAEFFER: SIMULTANÉ CAMEROUNAIS /

| NTRITTS-ARTEN | | |
|---|---|---|
| FÜR JEDES KONZERT | DM 3 | EINTRITTSKARTEN SIND AM EINGANG ZU ERHALTEN ODER DURCH: |
| FÜR EIN ABONNEMENT(14 KONZERTE) | DM 20 | VORVERKAUF  AM  HAUPTBAHNHOF  WIESBADEN |
| FÜR STUDENTEN | DM 1.50 | |

LUXUS * EINE INTERNATIONALE ZEITSCHRIFT NEUESTER KUNST ANTIKUNST MUSIK ANTIMUSIK DICHTUNG  ANTIDICHTUNG ETC

DICK HIGGINS
**Danger Music No. 2,** 1962
Performance at **Fluxus Internationale Festspiele Neuester Musik,** Wiesbaden 1962 (Photo Hartmut Rekort)

GEORGE MACIUNAS, DICK HIGGINS, WOLF
VOSTELL, BENJAMIN PATTERSON, EMMETT
WILLIAMS

performing Philip Corner's **Piano Activities** at **Fluxus
Internationale Festspiele Neuester Musik,** Wiesbaden
1962 (Photo Hartmut Rekort)

71 **Festum Fluxorum Fluxus/Musik og Anti-Musik/ Det Instrumentale Teater,** November 23-28, 1962
Nikolai Kirke, Copenhagen
Poster
83 x 61 cm

72 **Festum Fluxorum, Poesie, Musique et Antimusique, Evènenementielle et Concrète,**
December 3-8, 1962
American Students & Artists Center, Paris
Poster program designed by George Maciunas
32,5 x 23 cm

73 **Festum Fluxorum Fluxus/Musik und Antimusik/ Das Instrumentale Theater**
Staatliche Kunstakademie Düsseldorf,
February 2-3, 1963
Poster
48 x 23,5 cm

74 **Fluxus Festival/Theatre Compositions/Street Compositions/Exhibits/Electronic Music,**
June 23, 1963
Hypokriterion Theater, Amsterdam, and June 28, 1963,
Bleijenburg 16, Den Haag
Poster
85 x 61 cm

75 **A Little Festival of New Music,** London,
Goldsmiths' College, July 6, 1963
Handmade poster on newsprint
50 x 32 cm

76 **Items from Sissor Bros. Warehouse (Blink Show)**
(George Brecht, Alison Knowles, and Robert Watts)
Rolf Nelson Gallery, Los Angeles,
October 7 - November 2, 1963
Poster
41 x 33 cm

77 **Street Events** a part of „Fully Guaranteed 12 Fluxus Concerts", also called „Fluxus Festival at Fluxhall",
March-May 1964, New York City
George Maciunas' photograph of Dick Higgins, Lette Eisenhauer, Daniel Spoerri, Alison Knowles, and Ay-O sitting under a sign announcing „Street Events"
The photograph was intended to be used as a poster
51 x 41 cm

78 **Actions/AgitPop/Dé-Coll/age/Happening/ Events/Antiart/ L'Autrisme/Art Total/Refluxus,**
July 20, 1964,
Auditorium Maximum Aachen
Poster designed by Wolf Vostell, using an artwork by Nam June Paik
59 x 85 cm

79 **Actions/AgitPop/Dé-Coll/age/Happening/ Events/Antiart/ L'Autrisme Art Total/Refluxus,**
July 20, 1964,
Auditorium Maximum Aachen
Program publication with 32 pages by Tomas Schmit and Wolf Vostell
29,5 x 21 cm

80 **Fluxus Symphony Orchestra in Fluxus Concert,**
June 27, 1964
Carnegie Recital Hall, New York
Poster designed by George Maciunas
59 x 46 cm

81 **Perpetual Fluxus Festival,** Washington Square Gallery, 1964/65
Fluxus Edition
Poster designed by George Maciunas
44 x 41 cm

82 **Fluxorchestra at Carnegie Recital Hall,**
September 25, 1965
Carnegie Recital Hall, New York City
Program designed by George Maciunas
43 x 30 cm

83 **Fluxorchestra at Carnegie Recital Hall,**
September 25, 1965
Carnegie Recital Hall, New York City
Program designed by George Maciunas,
folded into a paper-airplane for delivery from the stage to the audience

84 **Fluxshop/Fluxorchestra,** includes **Fluxmanifesto on Fluxamusement,** ca. September 1965
Fluxus Edition
Handout designed by George Maciunas
53 x 17 cm

79

81

FLUXUS HQ P.O.BOX 180 NEW YORK 10013
FLUXSHOPS AND FLUXFESTS IN NEW YORK
AMSTERDAM NICE ROME MONTREAL TOKYO
V-TRE-FLUXMACHINES-FLUXMUSICBOXES
FLUXKITS-FLUXMACHINES-FLUXPOST
FLUXMEDICINES-FLUXFILMS-FLUXMENUS
FLUXRADIOS-FLUXORGANS-FLUXPUZZLES
FLUXCLOTHES-FLUXCARDS-FLUXSHIRTS
FLUXBOXES-FLUXORCHESTRA-FLUXJOKES
FLUXGAMES-FLUXHOLES-FLUXHARDWARE
FLUXSUITCASES-FLUXCHES-FLUXFLAGS
FLUXTOURS-FLUXWATER-FLUXCONCERTS
FLUXMYSTERIES-FLUXBOOKS-FLUXMAGIC
FLUXCLOCKS-FLUXCIRCUS-FLUXANIMALS
FLUXQUIZZES-FLUXWATER-FLUXMEDALS
FLUXDUST-FLUXCANS-FLUXTABLECLOTH
FLUXVAUDEVILLE-FLUXTAPE-FLUXSPORT
GENPEI AKASEGAWA-ERIC ANDERSEN-AYO-
GEORGE BRECHT-STANLEY BROUWN-ANT-
HONY COX-GIUSEPPE CHIARI-PHILIP COR-
NER-WALTER DE MARIA-WILLEM DE RID-
DER-ROBERT FILLIOU-DICK HIGGINS-HI-
RED CENTER-JOE JONES-ALISON KNOWLES
JIRI KOLAR-ARTHUR KOPCKE-TAKEHISA
KOSUGI-SHIGEKO KUBOTA-FREDERIC LIEB-
ERMAN-GYORGI LIGETI-JACKSON MAC LOW
GEORGE MACIUNAS-JONAS MEKAS-BARBA-
RA MOORE-ROBERT MORRIS-LADISLAV NO-
VAK-YOKO ONO-NAM JUNE PAIK-BENJAMIN
PATTERSON-JAMES RIDDLE-DITER ROT-
TAKAKO SAITO-WILLEM SCHIPPERS-TOMAS
SCHMIT-CHIEKO SHIOMI-DANIEL SPOERRI
BEN VAUTIER-ROBERT M.WATTS-EMMETT
WILLIAMS-LA MONTE YOUNG AND OTHERS

FLUXMANIFESTO ON FLUXAMUSEMENT-VAUDEVILLE-ART? TO ESTABLISH ARTIST'S NONPROFESSIONAL, NONPARASITIC, NONELITE STATUS IN SOCIETY, HE MUST DEMONSTRATE OWN DISPENSABILITY, HE MUST DEMONSTRATE SELFSUFFICIENCY OF THE AUDIENCE, HE MUST DEMONSTRATE THAT ANYTHING CAN SUBSTITUTE ART AND ANYONE CAN DO IT. THEREFORE THIS SUBSTITUTE ART-AMUSEMENT MUST BE SIMPLE, AMUSING, CONCERNED WITH INSIGNIFICANCES, HAVE NO COMMODITY OR INSTITUTIONAL VALUE. IT MUST BE UNLIMITED, OBTAINABLE BY ALL AND EVENTUALLY PRODUCED BY ALL. THE ARTIST DOING ART MEANWHILE, TO JUSTIFY HIS INCOME, MUST DEMONSTRATE THAT ONLY HE CAN DO ART. ART THEREFORE MUST APPEAR TO BE COMPLEX, INTELLECTUAL, EXCLUSIVE, INDISPENSABLE, INSPIRED. TO RAISE ITS COMMODITY VALUE IT IS MADE TO BE RARE, LIMITED IN QUANTITY AND THEREFORE ACCESSIBLE NOT TO THE MASSES BUT TO THE SOCIAL ELITE.

# CONDITIONS FOR PERFORMING FLUXUS PUBLISHED COMPOSITIONS, FILMS & TAPES

A. These conditions apply to the following:

complete works of: GEORGE BRECHT
               ALBERT M. FINE (textual work only)
               HI RED CENTER
               MILAN KNIŽAK
               GEORGE MACIUNAS
               CHIEKO SHIOMI
               JAMES RIDDLE
               BEN VAUTIER
               ROBERT WATTS

individual works of: ERIC ANDERSEN -     opus 50
               GIUSEPPE CHIARI -   La Strada
               ALISON KNOWLES -  Child art piece
               TAKEHISA KOSUGI - Anima I , Anima 2
                                          Chironomy 1, Ear drum event, For mr.M,
                                          Malika 5, Manodharma with Mr.T,  Manodharma with Mr.Y,
                                          Micro 1,  Music for a revolution,  Organic music,
                                          Tender Music,  Theatre Music.
               GYORGI LIGETI -    Poeme Symphonique (for 100 metronomes) 1962
                                            Trois Bagatelles, 1961
               JACKSON MAC LOW - Tree Movie
                                          Piano Suite for David Tudor and John Cage, 1961
                                          Punctuation mark numbers,
                                          One hundred,
                                          Thanks I, Thanks II,
                                          Letters for Iris, numbers for silence.
               BENJAMIN PATTERSON- Overture,
                                          Septet from "Lemons",
                                          Solo dance from "Lemons",
                                          Variations for double-bass,
                                          Traffic Light - a very lawful dance,
                                          Pond.
               NAM JUNE PAIK -    Zen for film.
               TOMAS SCHMIT -    Sanitas numbers: 2, 13, 22, 35, 107, 165,
                                          Zyklus for water pails,
                                          3 piano pieces for G.M.
                                          Floor and foot theatre.
               EMMETT WILLIAMS - Voice piece for La Monte Young
                                          Song of uncertain length,
                                          Litany and response ,
                                          Ten arrangements for 5 performers,
                                          Duet for performer(s) and audience,
                                          Counting songs numbers 1 to 6,
                                          A german chamber opera for 38 marias,
                                          Tag  and  An Opera.
               LA MONTE YOUNG - Trio for strings,
                                          1961 compositions.

B. BASIC CONDITION:
    1. If Fluxus compositions outnumber numerically or exceed in duration other, non-fluxus compositions
       in any concert, the whole concert must be called and advertised as FLUXCONCERT.
    2. If Fluxus compositions do not exceed non-fluxus compositions, the following notice must follow
       each Fluxus composition: BY PERMISSION OF FLUXUS   or
                                        FLUX-PIECE

C. ALTERNATE CONDITION:
    1. If basic condition is not followed, $ 50 fee must be paid to each applicable composer through
       Fluxus, for each composition performed.
    2. If compositions are announced or advertised but not performed the fee shall be $ 10 for each
       composition so announced.

Non compliance with any of the heretofore mentioned conditions by the producer(s) and/or performer(s)
will make him, her or them liable to a suit in court of Law for the recovery of amounts mentioned in
alternate condition.

85 **Conditions for Performing Fluxus Published Compositions, Films & Tapes,** n.d., ca. 1965
Fluxus Edition
Mimeographed text by George Maciunas, 1 page
35,5 x 21,5 cm

86 **Fluxus, or Fluxatlas . . . ,** 1966/67
Fluxus note-paper, designed and printed by George Maciunas
1 sheet
25,5 x 29 cm

87 **Fluxfest Sale,** special print, extract of 'Film-Culture', No. 43, Winter 1966 (ca. January 1967)
1 page, designed by George Maciunas
56 x 43 cm

88 **Fluxfest presents John and Yoko** at (Joe Jones' Tone Deaf Music Store, later at 80 Wooster Street) New York, April 11 - May 14, May 16 - 30, June 6 - 12, 1970
Poster designed by George Maciunas
41 x 43 cm

89 **Flux Games Flux Vehicle Day,** May 19, 1973
New York City
Mechanical designed by George Maciunas for the flyer
25,5 x 19 cm

90 DICK HIGGINS
**Invocation of Canyons and Boulders,** 1964
Fluxus Edition
Sheet of uncut images to be used for a flip book version of the work
Offset print
26 x 36 cm

91 HI RED CENTER
**Canned Mystery,** 1964
Made by Hi Red Center, distributed by Fluxus
This copy designated 'S-2' which refers to contents
Resealed tin can with handwritten notation, containing an unknown hard object. Offset „!" label.
6,7 cm diameter x 8 cm high

92 HI RED CENTER (GENPEI AKASEGAWA)
Prototype for **Bundle of Events,** early 1960's
Unique, made by Genpei Akasegawa
Paper and twine
16 x 7 x 7,5 cm

93 HI RED CENTER
**Bundle of Events,** 1965
Fluxus Edition, assembled by George Maciunas ca. 1966
Crumpled printed publication, black on grey-green paper, and twine
14 x 10 x 4 cm

94 HI RED CENTER
**Bundle of Events,** 1965
Edited by Shigeko Kubota, designed by George Maciunas, Fluxus Edition
1 sheet printed both sides, black on grey-green paper
56 x 43 cm

92

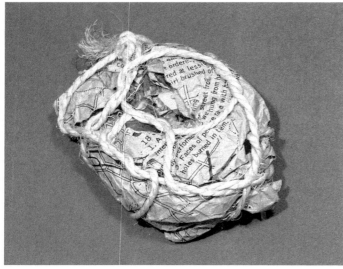

93

91

**95   HI RED CENTER**

**„!" (Exclamation point),** 1966
Fluxus Edition
Black and red cloth flag with metal grommets
73 x 73 cm

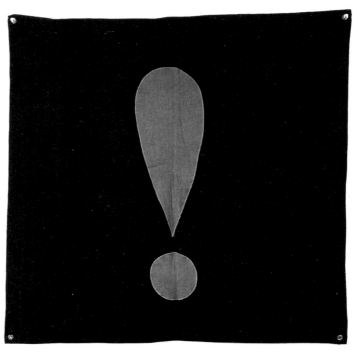

95

**96   HI RED CENTER**

**Street Cleaning Event,** June 1966
Grand Army Plaza (58th & 5th Ave.) New York City
3 Photographs by George Maciunas
51 x 41 cm each

96 a

96 b

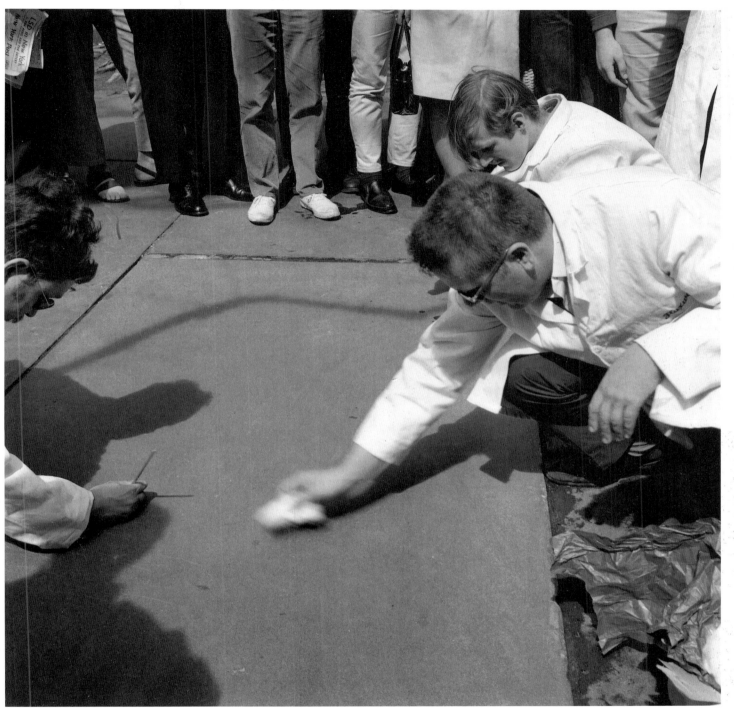

96 c

97 TOSHI ICHIYANAGI

**Music for Piano No. 7,** March 1961/1963
10 original score sheets handdrawn and typewritten
by George Maciunas for the Fluxus Edition after Toshi
Ichiyanagi's original manuscript
1 blueprint instruction sheet, Fluxus Edition
appr. 42 x 29 cm - score sheets
29,5 x 21 cm - instruction sheet

98 JOE JONES

**Flux Music Box,** 1965
Fluxus Edition, assembled by George Maciunas
Plastic box, altered music box works, and metal turn
keys
3 x 12 x 9 cm

99 JOE JONES

**Mechanical Fluxorchestra,** ca. 1966
Fluxus Edition, unique, assembled by George Maciunas
Guitar, bell, 2 aerophones, electric motors, wires, metal
stands, elastic and beaters
appr. 100 x 100 x 135 cm

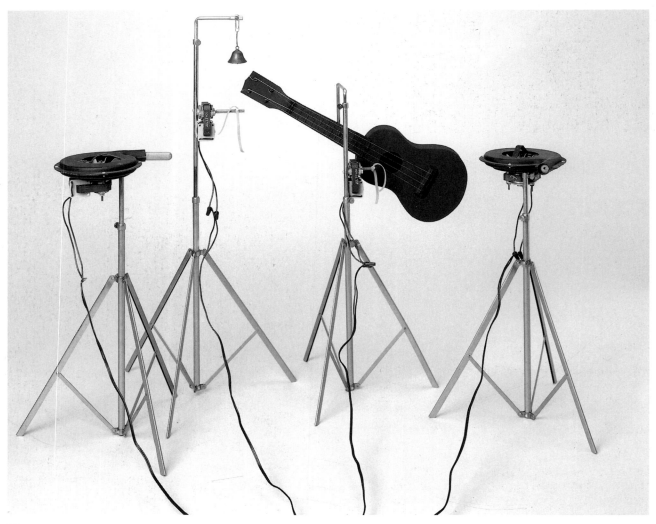

99

101

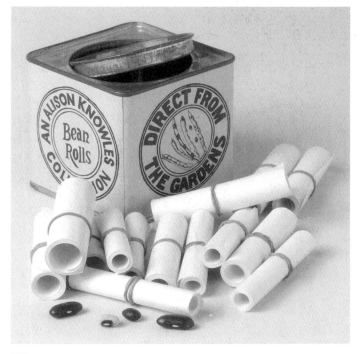

103

102　ALISON KNOWLES

**Music by Alison,** performed May 23, 1964 by Alison Knowles and Ben Vautier during „Fluxus Street Theatre" as a part of „Fully Garanteed 12 Fluxus Concerts", also called „Flux Festival at Fluxhall", New York City
Photograph by George Maciunas
51 x 40,5 cm

103　ALISON KNOWLES

**Bean Rolls,** 1964
Fluxus Edition
Tin can containing 12 scrolls and 3 dried beans
8 x 8 x 8 cm

104　ALISON KNOWLES

**Identical Lunch**
George Maciunas' score for his version of Knowles' **Identical Lunch** on a postcard, dated November 5, 1971
8,5 x 14 cm

100　JOE JONES

**Two Worms Chasing Each Other,** 1969/ca. 1977
Fluxus Edition, assembled by George Maciunas
Wood box containing painted metal toy (label on inside of lid)
appr. 7 x 17 x 16 cm

101　JOE JONES

**The Music Store,** New York, February 12, 1971
Invitation and program designed by George Maciunas
1 sheet
28 x 21,5 cm

102

6

105.  ARTHUR KOEPCKE

**(Surprises, Cheerups, Summons)**, ca. 1964
Possible prototype for Fluxus Edition, made by Arthur
Koepcke incorporating a Maciunas designed label
Empty plastic box with collaged label, unique
9,5 x 12 x 3 cm

106  ARTHUR KOEPCKE

**What's The Time,** 1969
Altered watch clock, sand timer, rubber stamped and
printed labels, mounted on wood
16,5 x 60,5 x 18 cm

107

108

107   TAKEHISA KOSUGI

**Anima I,** performed May 23, 1964 by Alison Knowles
and Ben Vautier during „Fluxus Street Theatre" part of
„Fully Guaranteed 12 Fluxus Concerts", also called „Flux
Festival at Fluxhall", New York City
Photograph by George Maciunas
51 x 40,5 cm

108   TAKEHISA KOSUGI
**Anima I**

&

BEN VAUTIER
**Attaché de Ben**

&

GEORGE MACIUNAS
**Solo for Violin**
Simultaneous performance, May 23, 1964, by Ben
Vautier (and Alison Knowles not pictured here) during
„Fluxus Street Theatre" during „Flux Festival at
Fluxhall", New York City
Photograph by George Maciunas
51 x 40,5 cm

109   TAKEHISA KOSUGI

**Events,** 1964
Fluxus Edition
Plastic box containing 12 printed cards
1,5 x 12 x 9,5 cm

110   SHIGEKO KUBOTA

**Letter to George Maciunas,** before June 20, 1964
Calligraphic letter and photograph on rice paper
95,5 x 27,5 cm

111   SHIGEKO KUBOTA

**Vagina painting,** Performed July 4, 1965, by the artist
during „Perpetual Fluxus Festival", Cinematheque 85 E.
4th Street, New York City
Photograph by George Maciunas
51 x 40,5 cm

112   SHIGEKO KUBOTA

**Flux Napkins,** 1967
Fluxus Edition, assembled by George Maciunas
Plastic box with 3 red paper napkins, and
collage elements
1,4 x 12 x 9 cm

109

111

Distribution:

George Brecht     Robert Watts     Nam June Paik
Henry Flynt     La Monte Young     Toshi Ichiyanagi
Dick Higgins     Walter De Maria.     Yoko Ono
Allan Kaprow
Jackson Mac Low     Emmett Williams
Richard Maxfield     Daniel Spoerri
Jonas Mekas     Robert Filliou
Bob Morris     Ben Vautier.
Ben Patterson     Tomas Schmit.
Stan Vanderbeek

## FURTHER PROPOSALS FOR N.Y.C. FLUXUS.
### FROM TOMAS SCHMIT:   PREFESTIVAL ACTIVITIES:

1. Change names & titles on concert posters etc., for instance... "today in town hall — Quintet in G major by (Emmett Williams)" or ... "today in Metropolitan opera - (FLUXUS) by R. Wagner" etc. etc. This change can be affected by pasting preprinted labels.

2. Attach or paste cards to buildings, automobiles, trees etc, saying for instance... "this is a danger music by Dick Higgins" & or "poem by Tomas Schmit" etc, etc.

3. On the day before the festival post an immense number of posters inscribed : "to-day is no day! tomorrow will be the fifth of November!"(if concert is to start on 5 th.) or " tomorrow will be FLUXUS day ! "

4. On the day of the opening concert call all museums, theatres, concert halls etc., by phone, anonymously, saying : "there is a time-bomb in your facility!" Little packages, well hidden & containing a card inscribed "bomb!" should be deposited in these locations, — In this way all museums, theatres, halls etc, would be closed for the evening, the anniversary of which would be celebrated as Fluxus day through the comming years.

### GRAND FLUXUS FESTIVAL

1.st. evening : one performer, announcing "the first evening of the Grand Festival will be tomorrow evening" exit. (G.M. piece)
2nd. evening : a bus (or boat) carries the audience beyond the city and deposits them there, returning empty. (T.Schmit composition
3rd. evening: people get free tickets for the fourth evening.— exit.
4th. evening: doors open, but no performers. (La Monte Young - comp.).
5th. evening: one performer in policeman's uniform announces: "this performance was forbidden by government!" exit.
6th. evening: doors of theatre are locked-up, an immense noise is to be heard from inside (tape recorded hand clapping, music, shouting, noises etc.).
7th. evening: one performer announces: "next performance will be tomorrow in Carnegie Hall",

### FROM NAM JUNE PAIK:  STREET COMPOSITIONS, & MOVING THEATRE - fluxus fleet.

1. Fluxus hero or heroine : (dedicated to Frank Trowbridge) — piss on the subway track & stop thus the train.
2. Zen for the street: adult in lotus posture & eyes half shut positions himself in a child carriage (perambulator) and is pushed by another adult or several children through shopping center or calm street.
3. Dragging suite : drag by a string along streets, stairs, floors: large or small dolls, naked or clothed dolls, broken, bloody, or new dolls, real man or woman, musical instruments, etc, etc.
4. 2 uniformed men wearing gas masks carry on a stretcher an "atom bomb victim" (a woman) half of the body prepared in a manner of cruel wounds & deformations, the other half in a sex-tease.
5. 100 meter running race in a very crowded downtown street.
6. MOVING-THEATRE (Fluxus fleet of cars & trucks) some activities mentioned by Paik in newsletter 6, others not yet disclosed.

### FROM HENRY FLYNT :

Last culminating festival event, in largest hall, largest audience — a lecture by Henry Flynt : denouncing all Fluxus festival activities as decadent serious culture aspects & expounding his BREND doctrine & campaign.

### FROM JACKSON MAC LOW:

1. Integration of Fluxus festival with political activities such as :
Support of a). Strikers & locked-out workers
      b). Walks for peace
Denunciation & agitation against:
      a). War in Vietnam
      b). US agression towards Cuba
      c). Nuclear testing
      d). Racial segregation & discrimination
      e). Capital punishment etc, etc, etc.....
In General: association with positive social action & activities, _never_ with antisocial, terroristic activities such as sabotage activities proposed in newsletter 6.

Newsletter 6, seems to have caused considerable misunderstanding among several recepients. This newsletter 6 was _not_ intended as a decision, settled plan or dictate, but rather - as a synthetic proposal or rather a signal, stimulus to start a discussion among, and an invitation for proposals from - the recepients (which it did - partly). The actual plan for Fluxus Festival will depend on the planning committee (after all proposals have been considered by all), and will be formalized most likely in September, since no enthusiasm was shown for activities to be carried out during Summer months.

George Maciunas

OUTLINES OF POLICY AND HISTORY OF
FLUXUS BY GEORGE MACIUNAS
(Nos. 113 - 116 )

113    GEORGE MACIUNAS

**Fluxus News-Policy Letter No. 6,** April 6, 1963
Ehlhalten, West Germany (Fluxus)
Vautier reprint, after April 6, 1963
Mimeo black on white paper, printed on the back of a
Ben Vautier announcement
30 x 21 cm

114    GEORGE MACIUNAS

**Fluxus News Letter No. 7,** May 1, 1963
Ehlhalten, West Germany (Fluxus)
Blueprint positive
30 x 21 cm

115    GEORGE MACIUNAS

**Diagram of Historical Development of Fluxus and
other 4 Dimensional, Aural, Optic, Olfactory,
Epithelial and Tactile Art Forms (Incomplete),** 1973
Black on white paper, compiled and designed by George
Maciunas
175,5 x 58,5 cm

INDIVIDUAL PIECES BY GEORGES MACIUNAS
(Nos. 116 - 125)

116    GEORGE MACIUNAS

**Music for Everyman,** November 1961
Score on parchment paper for Fluxus Edition, unique
125 x 30 cm

117    GEORGE MACIUNAS

**In Memoriam to Adriano Olivetti,**
November 8, 1962
Fluxus Edition
Blueprint on white paper
33,5 x 21 cm

118    GEORGE MACIUNAS

**12 Piano Compositions for Nam June Paik,**
January 2, 1962
**Solo for Balloons for J.P. Wilhelm,** January 3, 1962
**Solo for important man for Manfred De la Motte,**
January 3, 1962
Fluxus Edition
Blueprint score sheet (includes all 3 above scores)
29,5 x 21 cm

119    GEORGE MACIUNAS

**Homage to la Monte Young,** January 12, 1962
**Homage to Dick Higgins,** January 12, 1962
**Homage to Richard Maxfield,** January 12, 1962
**Homage to Walter De Maria,** January 13, 1962
**Homage to Jackson Mac Low,** January 14, 1962
5 typewritten scores on one sheet,
this version is possibly unique
36 x 16 cm

120    GEORGE MACIUNAS

**Grinderchess,** ca. 1965
Construction drawing for the wooden box
'Grinderchess', (George Maciunas based this work on an
idea of Takako Saito)
Ink on transparent paper
29,5 x 21 cm

121    GEORGE MACIUNAS

**Your Name Spelled With Objects,** 1972/ca. 1976
Fluxus Edition, assembled by George Maciunas
(Objects that spell out the name 'Jon Hendricks')
Blue plastic box with typewritten instructions on card,
containing a variety of glass, metal, and organic objects
5 x 10 x 12 cm

122    GEORGE MACIUNAS

**USA Surpasses All The Genocide Records!,**
ca. 1968
Distributed by Fluxus
Poster using the American red, white, and blue banner
Offset on white paper
54 x 88 cm

123    GEORGE MACIUNAS

**Fluxpost** (Aging Men), 1975
Fluxus Edition
Offset on gumed and perforated paper
28 x 22 cm

**HOMAGE TO LA MONTE YOUNG,** by George Maciunas,Jan.12,1962
(preferably to follow performance of any composition of 1961 by LMY.)

Erase,scrape or wash away as well as possible the previously drawn
line or lines of La Monte Young or any other lines encountered, like
street dividing lines, rulled paper or score lines, lines on sports fields,
lines on gaming tables, lines drawn by children on sidewalks etc.

**HOMAGE TO DICK HIGGINS,**      by George Maciunas, Jan.12,1962
(performance by Dick Higgins to last one year)

During the year of performance, do not create, compose anything  but
waltzes and marches for the policemens band.

**HOMAGE TO RICHARD MAXFIELD,** by George Maciunas,Jan.12,1962
(performance to follow performance of any tape composition of R.M.)
1. While rewinding the previously played master tape of R.Maxfield,
switch on the tape recorder the "erase" switch.
2. A chicken variation on the same theme:
just rewind the previously played tape of R.Maxfield without erasing.

**HOMAGE TO WALTER DE MARIA,** by George Maciunas,Jan.13,1962

Bring all boxes of Walter de Maria, including the 4ft.x 4ft. x 8ft. box to
performance area by the most difficult route, like via crowded subway or
bus, through skylight, window or fire escape; and then take them  back
same way as soon as they are brought in.

119

GEORGE MACIUNAS

**In Memoriam to Adriano Olivetti,** performed July 26,
1963, during the „Fluxus Festival of Total Art and
Comportment", Nice (Photo Phillipe François)

130

124  GEORGE MACIUNAS

**Fluxpost** (Smiles), 1978
Fluxus Edition
Offset on gumed and perforated paper
29 x 22 cm

125  GEORGE MACIUNAS

**Excreta Fluxorum,** Flux Science Show version
(each sample offered for sale separately), ca. 1972, this
version was assembled in 1977
Fluxus Edition, unique, each sample assembled by
George Maciunas. The entire collection of specimens
was placed later in a case designed by Larry Miller,
ca. 1985
appr. 13 x 84 x 53 cm

GEORGE MACIUNAS: DESIGN AND
ADVERTISING FOR FLUXUS EDITIONS AND
OTHER PUBLICATIONS (Nos. 126 - 131)

126   GEORGE MACIUNAS

**Theatrum Instrumentorum,** ca. 1961
Stationary, using a print of Albrecht Dürer
30 x 16 cm

127   GEORGE MACIUNAS

**Baroque Instrument String Catalog,** ca. 1961
E. & O. Mari, Inc., New York
Catalog designed for a commercial company
24 x 20,5 cm

128   GEORGE MACIUNAS

**An Anthology,** 1962
Folded-object designed by George Maciunas to
announce 'An Anthology', ed. by La Monte Young,
published by Jackson Mac Low and La Monte Young,
New York 1963. This cube was distributed at the first
Fluxus event, Wuppertal, June 9, 1962
Fluxus Edition
6,7 cm each side

129   GEORGE MACIUNAS

Staged photograph to be used for an advertisement of
the **Fluxshop & Mail Order Warehouse,**
359 Canal Street, New York City, April 10 to May 30,
1964
Pictured from bottom: Daniel Spoerri, Alison Knowles,
Dick Higgins, Ay-O, Lette Eisenhauer and George
Maciunas on sidewalk
51 x 40,5 cm

130   GEORGE MACIUNAS

**Seven Appendices** from Henry Flynt and George
Maciunas' **Communists Must Give Revolutionary
Leadership in Culture and Seven Appendices,**
1966
Worldview Publishers N.Y., designed by George
Maciunas and distributed by Fluxus
Printed publication
43 x 86 cm

131   GEORGE MACIUNAS

**Labels for individual Fluxus Editions**
a – Ay-O **Flux Rain Machine**
b – Ay-O **Finger Box** (three on different colored
      papers)
c – John Chick **Flux Food**
d – **Fluxfilms**
e – Ken Friedman **A Flux Corsage**
f – Per Kirkeby **Flux Finger Sweater**
g – Milan Knizák **Flux Dreams**
h – Carla Liss **Travel Flux Kit**
i – Robert Watts **Flux Rock**
j – Robert Watts **A Flux Atlas**
each appr. 8 x 11 cm

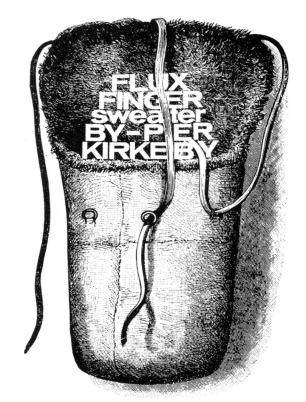

131 f

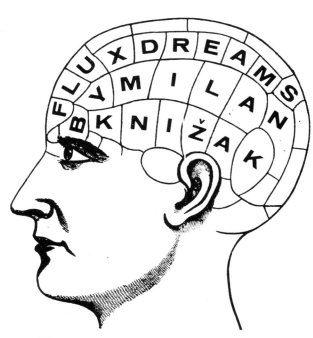

131 g

78

131 e

131 h

131 i

PETER MOORE
**Venetian Blinds,** ca. 1966 (Photo George Maciunas)

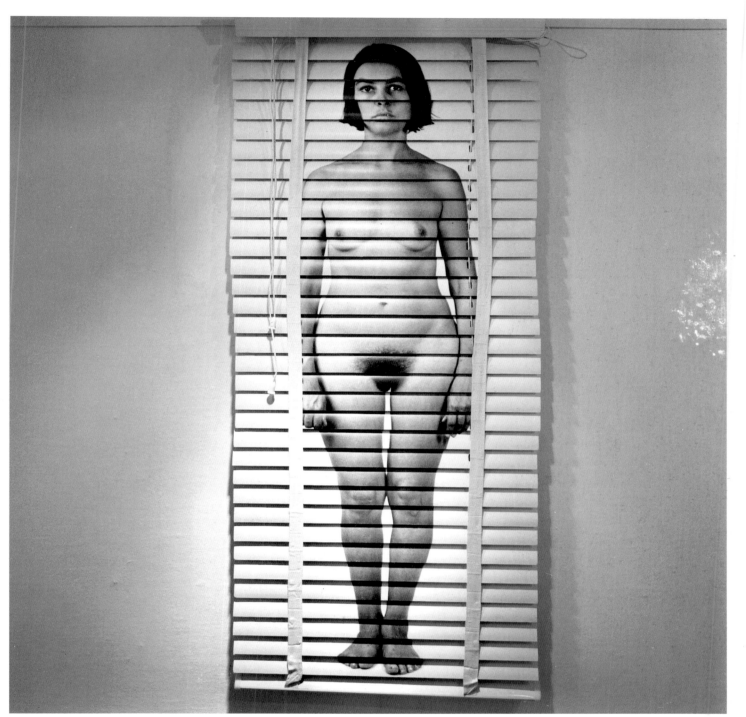

132 b

132   PETER MOORE
**Inverse Panoramic Portrait of Any Human
Subject,** Planned in 1966, possibly made in 1967
Fluxus Edition, made by the artist, unique
Photograph on material, wood and wire
179 x 87 cm

135

136

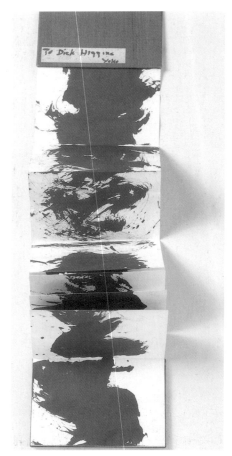

134

134  YOKO ONO

**Part Painting** „observe any section or sections as a complete and total painting", 1961, dedicated to Dick Higgins
Ink with stiff cover on paper
244 x 16 cm

135  YOKO ONO

**Paintings & Drawings by Yoko Ono,** July 17-30, 1961
Preview July 16, AG Gallery, New York City, entrance to the exhibtion
Photograph by George Maciunas
51 x 40,5 cm

136  YOKO ONO

**A Grapefruit in the World of Park,** November 24, 1961
Carnegie Recital Hall, New York City
Photograph by George Maciunas to be used as a poster
51 x 40,5 cm

137  YOKO ONO

**Piece for Nam June Paik, No. 1,** March 27, 1964
Original handwritten score
28 x 21,5 cm

138  YOKO ONO

**Grapefruit,** 1964
Wunternaum Press, Tokyo
Book
14 x 14 cm

133  CLAES OLDENBURG

**Rubber Udder, Heinz Catsup Bottle,** and possibly **Lorgnettes,** ca. 1965
Instruction drawing by George Maciunas for the Fluxus Edition, unique
Ink and pencil on paper
32 x 20 cm

138

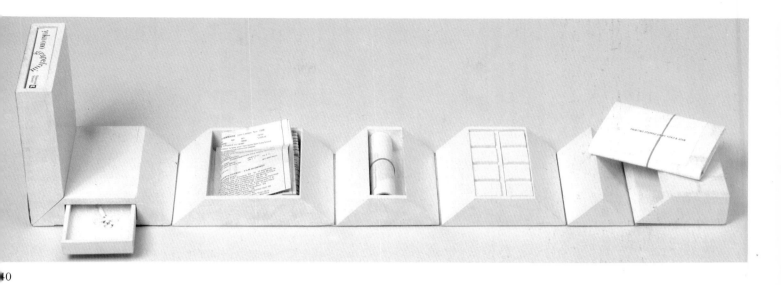

140

139 YOKO ONO

**Do it Yourself Fluxfest Presents Yoko Ono &
Dance Co.,** 1966
Mechanical by George Maciunas for the Fluxus edition
and its simultaneous appearence as a page in
„3 newspaper eVenTs for the pRicE of $1" (**Fluxus
Newspaper No. 7**), February 1, 1966
Collage
55 x 42 cm

140 YOKO ONO

**Everson Catalogue Box,** 1971
Includes works by Yoko Ono and John Lennon
Designed and produced by George Maciunas
Wood and vinyl sections containing assemblage,
footprints, glass key, plastic boxes, a book and printed
scores
15,5 x 15 x 18 cm unopened
4 x 15 x 94 cm opened

141 YOKO ONO

**Everson Catalogue Box,** 1971
Instruction drawing for the work by George Maciunas
Unique (2 sided)
25 x 31 cm

142 YOKO ONO

**This Is Not Here,** 1971
Everson Museum, Syracuse, New York
Designed by George Maciunas
Exhibition catalog and publication of works,
1 doublesheet, 4 pages
56 x 43 cm

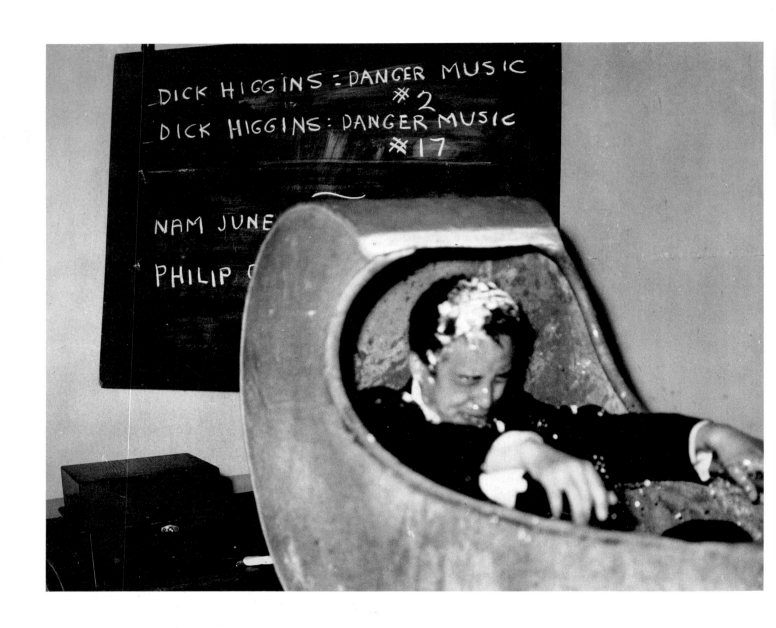

NAM JUNE PAIK

**Simple,** 1962
Performance at **Fluxus Internationale Festspiele Neuester
Musik,** Wiesbaden 1962 (Photo Hartmut Rekort)

NAM JUNE PAIK
at „Kleines Sommerfest ‚Après John Cage‘“, June 9, 1962
(Photo Rolf Jährling)

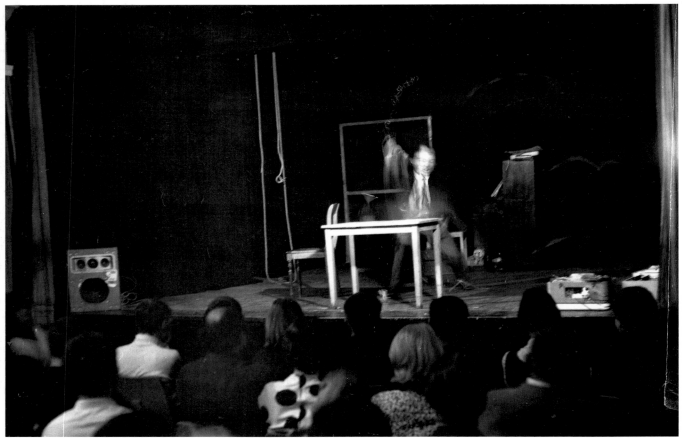

143 NAM JUNE PAIK

**One for Violin**
Performed by Paik during **Neo-Dada in der Musik,**
Düsseldorf, Germany, June 16, 1962
2 photographs by George Maciunas
25,5 x 20 cm each

144 NAM JUNE PAIK

**Exposition of Music (?),** Galerie Parnass, Wuppertal,
March 11-20, 1963
Invitation, program, poster, together with a text on
transparent paper by Nam June Paik and Jean Pierre
Wilhelm
25 x 35,5 cm

145 NAM JUNE PAIK

**Exposition of Music/Electronic Television,**
Galerie Parnass, Wuppertal, March 11-20, 1963
Poster
58 x 42 cm

146 NAM JUNE PAIK

Title unknown („**Violin with String"**), 1963
Photograph by Manfred Montwé
40 x 30,5 cm

147 NAM JUNE PAIK

**Fluxus Island in Décollage OCEAN,** 1963
Leaflet for the magazine **décoll|age** No. 4/63
40 x 57,5 cm

148 NAM JUNE PAIK

**Monthly Review of The University of Avantgarde
Hinduism,** 1963
Fluxus Edition, probably prepared for mailing by George
Maciunas and Tomas Schmit. Mailed work to Piero
Manzoni, returned to sender marked „morto", April 30,
1963
11 x 16 cm

149 NAM JUNE PAIK

**Monthly Review of The University for
Avantgarde Hinduism,** 1963
Fluxus Edition, made by the artist
Mailed work from Turkey to Tomas Schmit in Germany
9 x 14 cm

150 NAM JUNE PAIK

**Zen for Film,** 1964
Fluxus Edition
Plastic box containing 16 mm clear film leader loop
3 x 12 x 9 cm

151 NAM JUNE PAIK

**Zen for Film,** 1964/65
Fluxus Edition, made by the artist, unique
16 mm long version
Metal can with masking tape and handwritten titles,
containing film reel with approximately 20 minutes of
16 mm clear film leader
38 cm diameter

152 NAM JUNE PAIK

**Zen for TV,** 1963/1975
No. 4/12 made by the artist
Altered 19 inch black and white television set
58,5 x 41,5 x 36 cm

152

NAM JUNE PAIK (SEOUL, KOREA)
EXPOSITION OF MUSIC (?)
Electronic Television(?) Kindergarten der „Alten"?
How to be satisfied with 70%? Féticism of "idea"?
Erinnerung an das 20. Jahrhundert? objets sonores?
sonolized room? HOMMAGE à Rudolf Augstein?
Instruments for Zen-exercise? Prepared W. C.?
Bagatèlles americaines? etc? que sais-je?
Do it your . . . ? Freigegeben ab 18 Jahre?
Synchronisation als ein Prinzip akausaler Verbindungen?
A study of german Idiotology? Is the TIME without contents possible? etc?
Artistic Collaborator: Tomas Schmitt · Frank Trowbridge
Technic: Günther Schmitz (chief) · M. Zenzen (N. F.) · A. Schrage
Galerie Parnass
Wuppertal-Elberfeld
Moltkestr. 67 Tel. 35241
11. - 20. März 1963, 19.30 - 21.30 Uhr
Eintritt 5,- DM
Kartenvorbestellung ist wegen der beschränkten Plätze erbeten

144

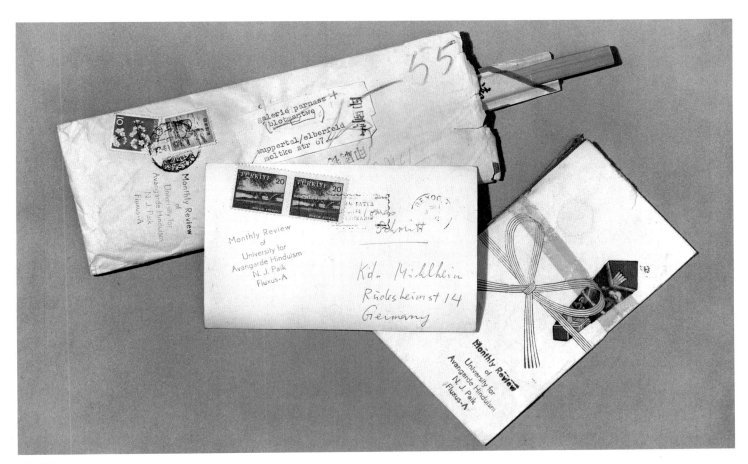

148/149

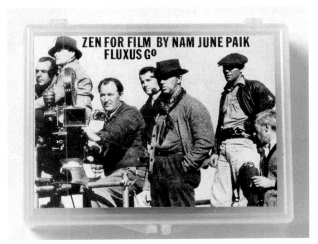

150

PAPER PIECE

5 performers

instrumentation:
    15 sheets of paper per performer approximate size o° standard news-
paper, quality varied, newspaper, tissue paper, light cardboard,
colored, printed or plain.
    3 ~~bags~~ paper bags per performer; quality, size and shape varied

duration:
    10 to 12½ minutes

procedure:
    A general sign from a chairman will begin the piece. Within the
following 30 seconds performers enter at will. The piece ends when
the paper supply is exhausted.

By each performer,
    7 sheets are performed
    SHAKE
    BREAK- opposite edges of the sheet are grasped firmly and sharply
           jerked apart
    TEAR- each sheet is reduced to particles less than 1/10 size of the
           original

    5 sheets are performed
    CRUMPLE
    RUMPLE
    BUMPLE- bump between hands

    3 sheets are performed
    RUB
    SCRUB
    TWIST- twist tightly to produce a squeaking sound

    3 bags are performed
    POOF- inflate with mouth
    POP!

dynamics are improvised within natural borders of approximate ppp of
TWIST and fff of POP!
each performer previously selects, arranges, materials and ~~seque~~
sequence of events. arrangement of sequence may concern not only
general order - sheet no. 1 SHAKE,BREAK, TEAR; no. 2 RUB, SCRUB
TWIST; no. 3 POOF, POP! - the inner order may also be considered-
TWIST, SCRUB, RUB. method of performance should be marked on each
sheet.

                                benjamin patterson
                                sept. 1960, köln

153

153  BENJAMIN PATTERSON

**Paper Piece,** 1960/1963
Fluxus Edition
Score, blueprint on white paper
23,5 x 21 cm

154  BENJAMIN PATTERSON

**Exposition à Paris,** July 3, 1962
Subtitled: Sneak Preview fluxus, happenings . . .
Printed with handwritten notes on wrapping paper
stamped „Galerie Légitime"
47 x 20 cm

155   JAMES RIDDLE

**One Hour,** 1966
Fluxus Edition
Printed black on white paper
56 x 44 cm

156   TAKAKO SAITO

**Portrait of Takako Saito with her Smell Chess,**
Winter 1964, New York City
Photograph by George Maciunas
51 x 41 cm

157   TAKAKO SAITO

**Game Box** („To George for your FLX Takako"),
ca. 1965
Prototype for a suggested Fluxus Edition, made by the
artist
Wooden box with handwritten notations packed with
small wooden boxes
13 x 14 x 24 cm

158   TAKAKO SAITO

**Game Box** (To Joe Jones: „For you and your children
you will have someday"), ca. 1965
Made by the artist
This **Game Box** is similar to the **Game Box** „To
George for your FLX Takako", although the contents
have been used and dispersed
Wooden box with loose small wooden boxes
13 x 14 x 24 cm

159   TAKAKO SAITO

**Fluxchess/Spice Chess,** ca. 1965/66
Fluxus Edition, assembled by George Maciunas
32 test tubes in grid, filled with spices, in a wooden box
14,5 x 17 x 20 cm

160   TAKAKO SAITO

**Ball Game,** ca. 1966
Fluxus Edition, constructed by the artist
Wooden game with glass sides and metal balls
8 x 9,5 x 9,5 cm

159

156

TOMAS SCHMIT
**Zyklus für Wassereimer (oder Flaschen)**
performed in Amsterdam 1963 (Photos Dorine van der Klei)

161   TOMAS SCHMIT

**Typewriter Poem,** March 1963
Unique handdrawn score
21 x 30 cm

< star piece >

The biggest star — Look at it while you like.
The second biggest star — Obscure it with smoke of a cigarette.
The third biggest star — Shoot it with a gun.
The fourth biggest star — Hold a cat in your arms.
The fifth biggest star — Look at it through a telescope.
The sixth biggest star — When you find it, look at your watch.
The seventh biggest star — Reflect it in the water of a glass
                          and drink it.
The eighth biggest star — Obscure it with flame of a candle.
The ninth biggest star — Draw a deep breath.
The tenth biggest star — Lie down and look it through a loop
                         of your fingers.
The eleventh biggest star —Read a letter sent to you recently.

    Do this piece on the roof of a building
    or in the park.

                                        C. Shiomi 1963

163

162  MIEKO (CHIEKO) SHIOMI
**Event for the Midnight,** 1963
Handwritten score, ink on paper
11 x 18 cm

163  MIEKO (CHIEKO) SHIOMI
**Star Piece,** 1963
Handwritten score, ink on paper
18 x 23 cm

164  MIEKO (CHIEKO) SHIOMI
**Events and Games,** 1964
Fluxus Edition
Plastic box containing printed scores and crumpled
photograph
1,5 x 18 x 13 cm

165  MIEKO (CHIEKO) SHIOMI
**Spatial Poem No. 1,** 1965
69 word locations indicated by printed flags pinned to a
handdrawn map on fiber board
39,5 x 39,5 cm

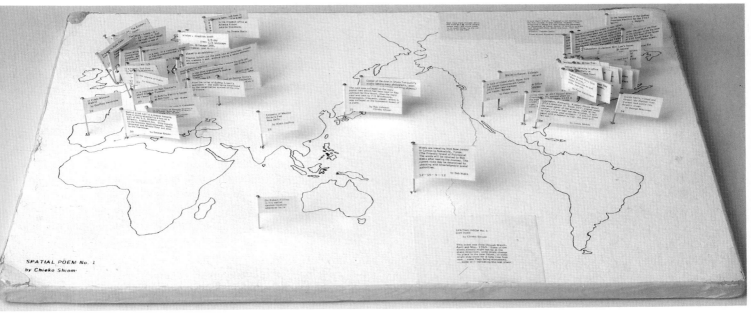

165

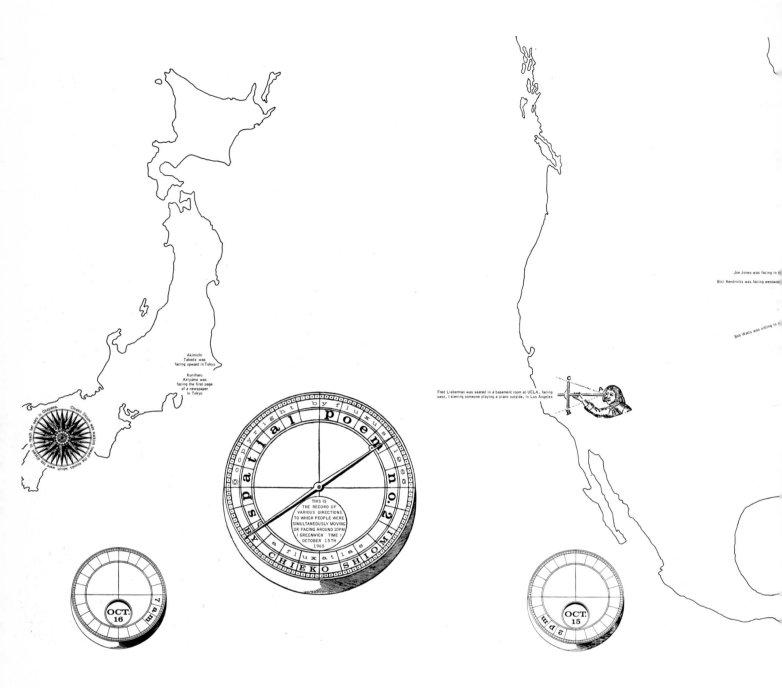

Akimichi
Takeda was
facing upward in Tokyo

Kuniharu
Akiyama was
facing the first page
of a newspaper
in Tokyo

Joe Jones was facing in
Bici Hendricks was facing westwar
Bob Watts was sitting in

Fred Lieberman was seated in a basement room at UCLA, facing
west, listening someone playing a piano outside, in Los Angeles

166

166   MIEKO (CHIEKO) SHIOMI
**Spatial Poem No. 2,** 1966
Fluxus Edition
Print on white paper
36,5 x 82,5 cm

167   MIEKO (CHIEKO) SHIOMI
**[Spatial Poem No. 3],** 1972
Postcard by George Maciunas to Mieko Shiomi
regarding production of **Spatial Poem No. 3,**
postmarked
March 16, 1972
8 x 14 cm

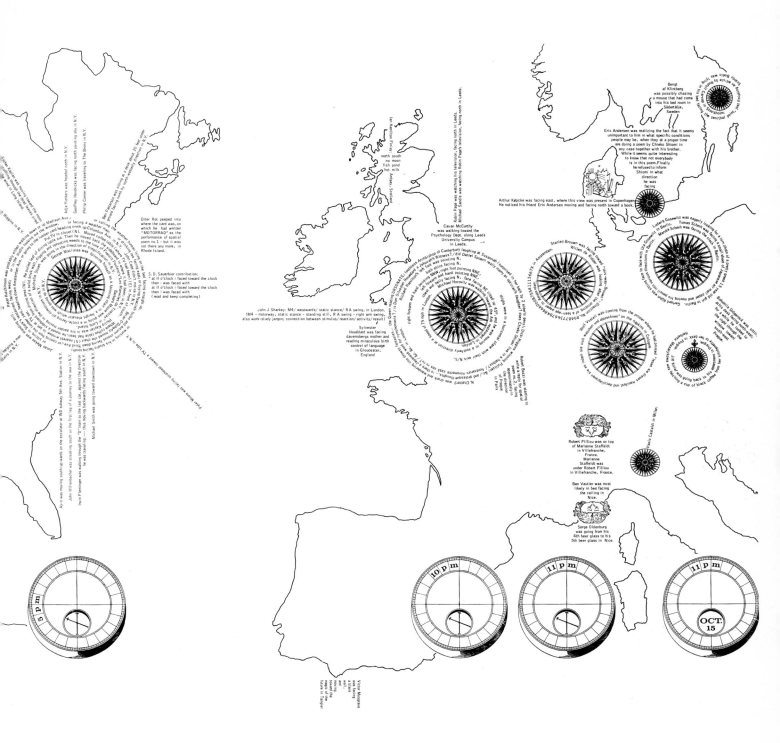

168   MIEKO (CHIEKO) SHIOMI

**Spatial Poem No. 3,** First advertised in 1966, but not
produced until 1972
Fluxus Edition, assembled by George Maciunas
Leather, metal bolts, and printed sheets
3 x 30 x 13 cm

169 DANIEL SPOERRI and FRANÇOIS DUFRENE

**L'Optique Moderne,** 1963
Fluxus Edition, typography by George Maciunas
Book
20 x 14 cm

170 DANIEL SPOERRI

**Altered Glasses,** n.d.
Made by the artist
Altered plastic framed glasses with metal needles
13 x 13 cm

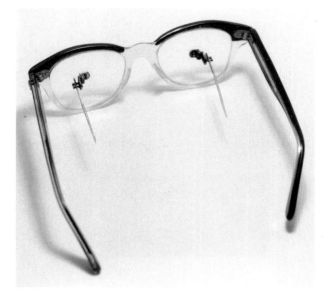

170

169

100

171 YASUNAO TONE
**Anagram for Strings,** 1963
Original handdrawn score by George Maciunas for the
Fluxus Edition after Yasunao Tone, and blueprint
instruction sheet
29 x 21 cm instruction sheet
21 x 30 cm score

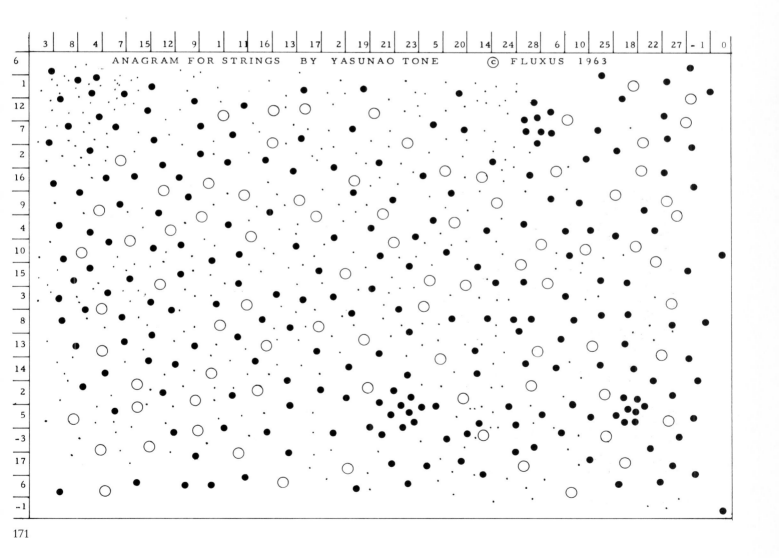

171

172  BEN VAUTIER

**Fluxcatalogue,** 1960/1973
As **Complete Works,** Ben Vautier started signing
reference books in 1960. This dictionary was offered to
Maciunas ca. 1973 as a prototype for a proposed Fluxus
Edition
which was not made
Unique, made by the artist
Altered dictionary
26 x 17,5 x 5,5 cm

173  BEN VAUTIER

**A Flux Suicide Kit,** 1962/reassembled 1984
Prototype made by the artist for the Fluxus Edition,
unique
Together with a unique 1984 plaque made by the artist,
regarding the work
Green cardboard and metal carrying case with
handwriting containing rope, shotgun shells, razor
blades, electrical plug and metal clamps
White painting on black painted wood
12 x 20 x 33 cm box
10 x 14 cm plaque

174  BEN VAUTIER

**Light Bulb,** 1962
A unique sculpture, made by the artist,
(the idea was given to Maciunas for a Fluxus Edition
which was never made) together with a unique
1984 plaque made by the artist regarding the work
Metal and glass light fiture with light bulb and cord
White painting on black painted wood
Sculpture 23,5 x 18,5 x 8 cm
Plaque 10 x 14 cm

175  BEN VAUTIER

**Signing of Certificates,** July 27, 1963
During **Fluxus Festival of Total Art and
Comportment,**
Nice, France
Photograph by George Maciunas
25,5 x 20,5 cm

176  BEN VAUTIER

**The Postman's Choice,** 1965
(2 items)
Fluxus Edition
Postcard, 1965
Fluxpostcard, 1967
8,5 x 14 cm each

174

177  BEN VAUTIER

**Assholes Wallpaper,** ca. 1973
Fluxus Edition
George Maciunas used frames from Yoko Ono's
**Film No. 4** (Bottoms) and attributed the work to
Vautier (it should be properly titled **Yoko Ono,
Bottoms Wallpaper**)
Printed black on white paper
56,5 x 43 cm
appr. 100 sheets

175

BEN VAUTIER
**Brosse à dents,** July 26, 1963
Performed during **Fluxus Festival of Total Art and
Comportment,** Nice (Photo by Phillipe François)

173

FLUX
POST
CARD

BY BEN, 1965 © 1967, BY FLUXUS

THE POSTMAN'S CHOICE
LE CHOIX DU FACTEUR

176

178  WOLF VOSTELL

**décoll|age, Bulletin aktueller Ideen, No. 1,** 1962
Köln, June 1962
First issue of Vostell's magazine with various
contributions by Fluxus artists
26 x 22 cm

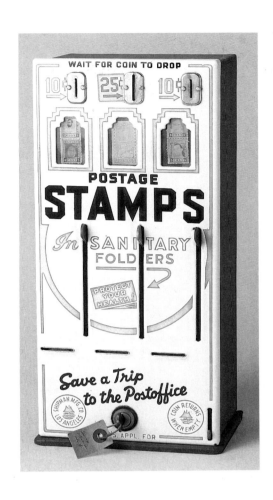

179  ROBERT WATTS
**Stamp Dispenser,** 1963
Stamp dispenser used for **Flux Post 17–17** and
**Yam Flug 5 Post 5** stamps
Altered readymade
40,5 x 19 x 13 cm

180

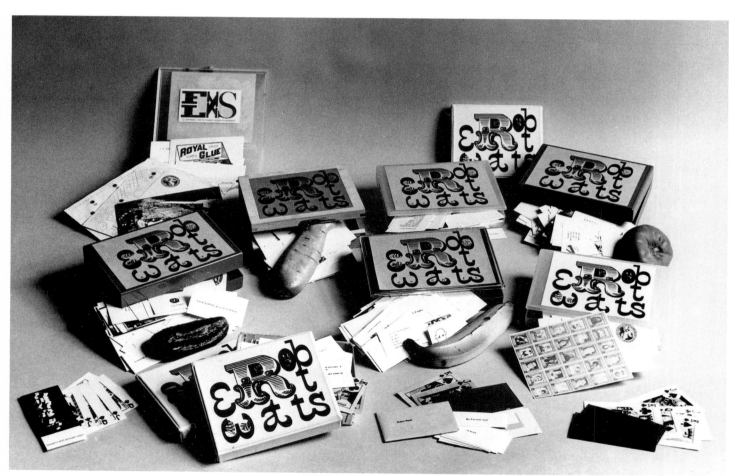

181/182

183

180  ROBERT WATTS
**Chromed Toothbrush,** 1964
Made by the artist
This is one of the **Chromed Goods** that would have
been included in a „handwritten" catalogue offered by
Fluxus, unique
1,5 x 1 x 15 cm

181  ROBERT WATTS
**Events,** 1964/65
Fluxus Edition
Transparent plastic box containing 57 scores printed on
white cards, including 3 sheets of stamps
3 x 18 x 13 cm

182  ROBERT WATTS
**Events,** 1964/date of assembly not known
Fluxus Edition, deluxe version assembled by George
Maciunas
Wooden box with brass hinges containing 94 scores
printed on white cards and plastic carrot
5 x 16,5 x 14 cm

183  ROBERT WATTS
**Flux Rock Marked by Volume in cc,** 1964
Fluxus Edition, assembled by George Maciunas
Wooden box with rock and presstype
10,5 x 10,5 x 10,5 cm

184  ROBERT WATTS
**Flux Timekit,** 1966/1978
Fluxus Edition, assembled by Brian Buczak and
Geoffrey Hendricks under the direction of
George Maciunas
Plastic box containing a variety of objects that have
a relationship to time duration in their use
6 x 33 x 21 cm

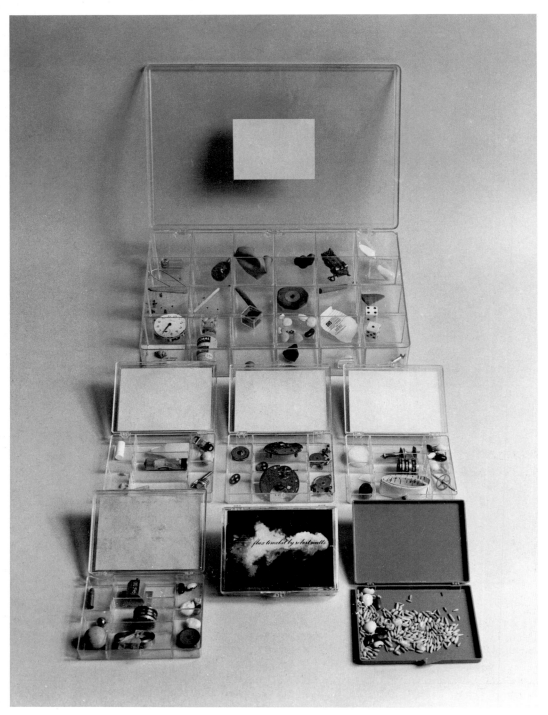

184

## 185 EMMETT WILLIAMS

**The Alphabet Symphony,** 1962
26 different photographs of a „Universal Poem" first
performed at Gallery One, London, during the **Festival
of Misfits.**
Photographs mounted on board, unique in this form,
taken by Bernard Kirchhoff at Studio Ordo,
Darmstadt 1963
40 x 64 cm (A)
40 x 60 cm (B, P)
40 x 57 cm (Y)
40 x 56 cm (K, V)
40 x 55 cm (H, J, C, R)
40 x 50 cm (M, S, T, X, Q)
40 x 30 cm (D, E, F, G, I, L, N, O, U, W, Z)

## 186 EMMETT WILLIAMS

**An Opera,** 1963
Published by Fluxus
Printed text on scroll
178 x 10 cm

## 187 EMMETT WILLIAMS

**Alphabeth Poem, (Long Poem),** ca. 1963
Published by Fluxus
Printed text on scroll
233 x 6 cm

### AN OPERA
#### by emmett williams

yes, it was still there. shutting his eyes would not make it flee once he opened them again. it had no father, no mother, yet there it was, just as he had conceived it between the unwritten sheets. he stroke it gently, then lifted it tenderly to the night table, where he placed it, without spilling a drop of its efficacy, plop in the middle of a folded kleenex. it was sweating, so he wiped it with his index finger. alas! the dot was gone. there was no mistaking it as he bent closer and saw the stump, the bare stump of the i without its had. it had lost itself in the grain of the wood. he sprang out of bed and switched on the overhead light. covering his nakedness from the newborn invalid with his left hand, he lifted everything off the table with his right and placed the objects, one by one, as they were on the tabletop, onto the bed. with his free hand he went over every inch of the tabletop. to no avail. he bent down and licked the table, licking from left to right, right to left, up and down and back again, slowly, then frantically, feverishly, in and out faster and faster, coating the surface with saliva and sweat. he pulled his tongue back in suddenly. he rushed up to the mirror and thrust it out. he could see nothing unusual. but the painful throbbing spread. he looked at it again. no dot. now his teeth hurt, too. his lower jaw. left ear. he fled to the end of the hall, where the young woman lived, and entered without knocking.

"wake . up . . wake . . . up . . . . , " he implored.

her left eye opened, then the right. "what do you want at this ungodly hour?"

                         "you . . . . . must . . . . . . come . . . . . . . with . . . .
. . . . me . . . . . . . . . quickly . . . . . . . . . . , " he pleaded.

"pull yourself together, man. get under the cover and catch a little sleep."

                       "but . . . . . . . . . . . you . . . . . . . . . . . .
must . . . . . . . . . . . . . come . . . . . . . . . . . . . . with . . . . . . . . . . . . . . . me . . . . . .
. . . . . . . . . . at . . . . . . . . . . . . . . . . . once . . . . . . . . . . . . . . . . . . "

"you can't be that hard up."

                               "you . . . . . . . .
. . . . . . . . . . don't . . . . . . . . . . . . . . . . . understand . . . . . . . . . . . . . . . . . . . .
. it's . . . . . . . . . . . . . . . . . . . . . my . . . . . . . . . . . . . . . . . . . . . tongue . . . . . . .
. . . . . . . . . . . . . . . . . my . . . . . . . . . . . . . . . . . . teeth . . . . . . . . .
. . . . . . . . . . . my . . . . . . . . . . . . . . . . . . . gums . . . . . . . . .
. . . . . . . . . my . . . . . . . . . . . . . . . . . . . left . . . . . . . . . . .
. . . . . . . . . . ear . . . . . . . . . . . . . . . . . . . . and . . . . . . . . . .
. . . . . . . . . . . it's . . . . . . . . . . . . . . . . . . . spreading . . .
. . . . . . . . . . . . . . . . . . . . . . . . to . . . . . . . . . . . . . . . . . . . . . . . . . .
. . . . my . . . . . . . . . . . . . . . . . . . . . throat . . . . . . . . . . . .
. . . . . . . . . . . . . . . help ! . . . . . . . . . . . . . . . . . . . . . . . .
me . . . . . . . . . . . . . . . . . . . . . . . . . . . . do . . . . . . . . . . . . . .
. . . . . . . . . . . . . . . something . . . . . . . . . . . . . . . . . . . . . . . .
. . . . . . pull . . . . . . . . . . . . . . . . . . . . . . . . . . it . . . . . . . . . .
. . . . . . . . . . . . . . pull . . . . . . . . . . . . out . . . . . . . . . . . . . . . . . . . .
. . . . . . . . . . . . . . . . . . . . . . . . . . . . . . . . . . . . . . . . . . . . . . . it
. . . . . . . . . . . . . . . . . . . . . . . . . . . . out . . . . . . . . . . . . . .
. . . . . . . . . . . . . . . . . please . . . . . . . . . . . . . . . . . . . . . . .
. . . . . . . . . . . . . . . . help . . . . . . . . . . . . . . . . . . . . . . . . . . . .
. . . . . . . . . me . . . . . . . . . . . . . . . . . . . . . . . . . . . . . . . . .
. "
"calm down a bit, for pity's sake. what is it you want me to pull out?"

     "look . . . . . . . . . . . . . . . . . . . . . . . . . . . . . . . . . . . . . . . . . at . . . . .
. . . . . . . . . . . . . . . . . . . . . . . . . . . . . . . . . . . . . . . . . . . . . it . . . . .
. . . . . . . . . . . . . . . . . . . . . . . . . . . . . . . . . do . . . . . . . . . . . . . . . .
. . . . . . . . . . . . . . . . . . . . . . . . you . . . . . . . . . . . . . . . . . . . . . . .
. . . . . . . . . . . . . . . . . . see . . . . . . . . . . . . . . . . . . . . . . . . . . . . . .
. . . . . . . . . . . . . . . . it . . . . . . . . . . . . . . . . . . . . . . . . . . . . . . . . .
. . . . . . . . . . . . . ? "

"i see a tongue, that's all i see. now look, i don't even know who you are. either cool off and get in bed with me for a little while or go back where you came from. i just hit the pad and i intend to get some more sleep." she rolled over and pulled the pillow over her head.

         "you're . . . . . . . . . . . . . . . . . . . . . . . . . . . . . . . . . . . . . . . .
. . . . . . . . . . . . . a . . . . . . . . . . . . . . . . . . . . . . . . . . . . . . . . . . . . . .
. . . . . . . . . murderer . . . . . . . . . . . . . . . . . . . . . . . . . . . . . . . .
. . . . . . . . . . . . . . "

a

b

c

d

e

f

186

g

h

i

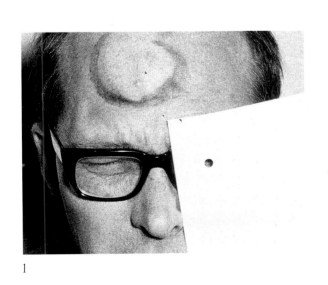

j

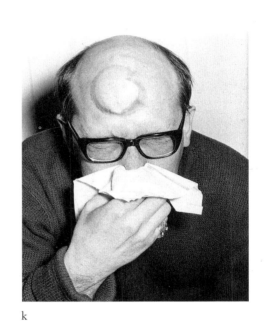

k

l

m

n

o

p

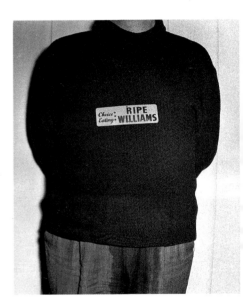

q

r

s

t

u

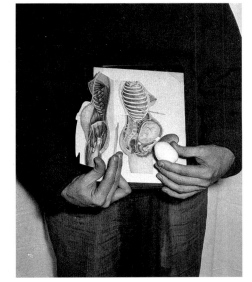

v

w

x

y

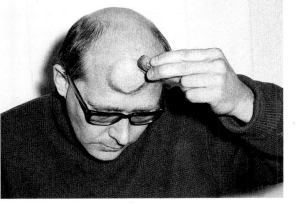

z

188   LA MONTE YOUNG
**Compositions 1961,** 1963
Published by Fluxus
Book
9 x 9 cm

188

189   LA MONTE YOUNG, Editor
**An Anthology,** 1963
Designed by George Maciunas, published by Jackson
Mac Low and La Monte Young, New York
First edition of the book
20,5 x 22,5 cm

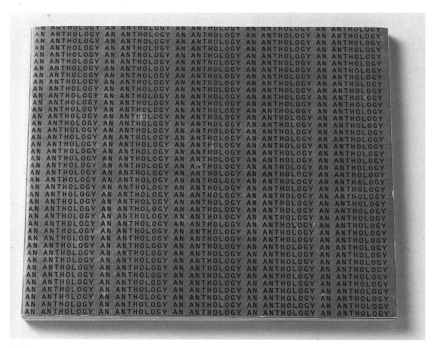

189

LA MONTE YOUNG

**The Tortoise Droning Selected Pitches From the Holy Numbers for the Two Black Tigers, the Green Tiger and the Hermit,** from: **The Tortoise, His Dreams and Journeys,** performed 1964 at the Pocket Theatre, New York (Tony Conrad, Marian Zazeela, La Monte Young and John Cale) (Photo by George Maciunas)

Jon Hendricks

## UNCOVERING FLUXUS – RECOVERING FLUXUS

*Reasons for our copyright arrangements;*

*1. Eventually we would destroy the <u>authorship</u> of pieces & make them totally anonymous – thus eliminating artists "ego"- Author would be "FLUXUS". We can't depend on each "artist" to destroy his ego. The copyright arrangement will eventually force him to it if he is reluctant.*
*2. When we hold copyright collectively we propagandize the collective rather than the individual.*
*3. When FLUXUS is noted after each FLUXUS copyrighted composition it helps to propagandize the broader-collective aspect of the composition...*

From a letter by George Maciunas to Tomas Schmit (ca. January, 1964).

George Maciunas came up with the word "Fluxus" to use as the name for the movement in July 1961. Some months before this, perhaps as early as October 1960, he had been engaged in plans to edit a literary magazine of expatriot Lithuanians called **Fluxus**. By March 1961 Maciunas announced a series of three lectures on "The significance in music of realism, concretism and fusion of form and content as opposed to bimorphic illusionism" at his Madison Avenue AG Gallery in New York. The flyer for the event stated: "Entry contribution of $3 will help to publish Fluxus magazine."

During July 1961 George Maciunas was working in New York City on the design and production of **An Anthology** which was edited by La Monte Young. Maciunas was also producing the final evening events in the series **Musica Antiqva et Nova** at the AG Gallery. The programs were: **Works by La Monte Young** on July 2 and 9; **Works by Henry Flynt** on July 15 and 16; **Works by Walter De Maria** on July 23; and **Nothing by Ray Johnson** on July 30.

Yoko Ono's exhibition "Paintings & Drawings" at the AG Gallery from July 16 to 30, 1961, was held simultaneously with the last three **Musica Antiqva et Nova** events and consisted most importantly of conceptual and participatory paintings. Visitors to the show were invited to take part in the realization or completion of the pieces. **Smoke Painting**, for example, could be burned with a cigarette or match by the visitor who could then watch the smoke rise and the canvas burn up. **Painting to be Stepped On** was a piece of canvas laid on the floor to be walked on.

Yoko Ono describes talking with Maciunas in July during her exhibition. He asked her to think of a word to call the movement he was hatching. Yoko Ono couldn't think of a name, and recalls being less interested in forcing grouping and labeling on artists, than in individually breaking away from the aesthetic and cultural controls that had been imposed on her as an artist, and as a woman. Undaunted, the next day he met her in the gallery and was very excited. She remembers him telling her the word "Fluxus" and then reading her the dictionary definition with its meanings of change and flow and the scatological meaning of excretion, areas that he was very interested in.

*FLUXUS*

*To purge. A fluid discharge, esp. an excessive discharge, from the bowels or other part. A continuous moving on or passing, as of a flowing stream, a stream; copious flow, the setting of the tide towards the shore. Any substance or mixture, as silicates, limestone and fluorite, used to promote fusion, esp. the fusion of metals or minerals.*

Fluxus...Tentative Plan for Contents of the first 7 Issues... (before January 18, 1962) Excerpt.

La Monte Young also remembers that it was in the summer of 1961 when he and Maciunas were standing on the corner of 6th Avenue and Houston Street in New York and Maciunas mentioned to him the word "Fluxus".

Yoko Ono's idea of license, the setting up of a situation where others could complete a work of art instead of the artist, was a radical departure from the existing concept of the role of the artist. It was to play an enormous part in Maciunas' own thinking and was to be the position he took in the future production of Fluxus works. This distance between the concept and the realization of a work is an inherent element in most Fluxus works.

Within a year he came into contact with Daniel Spoerri, whose independent, though more formal certificates for **Tableau-Piège, fabriqué sous licence par:...** of May 1962 reinforced Maciunas' notion of the dispensability of the artist.

The idea of producing Fluxus yearboxes of completely new, unpublished works by the most radical artists from many different countries  was derived from La Monte Young's idea for **An Anthology**. Initially Maciunas thought of a magazine in an expanded format to promote the movement. He had developed that idea by December 1961, planning six issues. By January 1962 this had changed to a projected seven "yearbooks".

*Enclosed is the latest plan for the forthcoming issues of Fluxus.*

*1. It was decided to utilize instead of covers a flat box to contain the contents so as to permit inclusion of many loose items: records, films, "poor man's films-flip books", "original art", metal, plastic, wood objects, scraps of paper, clippings, junk, raggs [sic]. Any compostition or work that cannot be reproduced in standard sheet form or cannot be reproduced at all.*
*2. Fluxus will be issued in 2 editions.*
*a) 1000 copies of standard edition which will contain only reproducible sheet or printable matter. This will consist of 150 8" x 8" bound pages and 12 loose sheets, fold outs or boards and will sell for $ 4.00 or its equivalent.*
*b) 200 copies of luxus-fluxus, which in addition of [sic] standard edition will contain several original solid-nonreproducible works: films, pieces of 2 dimensional or 3 dimensional art,*

BREVET DE GARANTIE

## TABLEAU - PIÈGE

Fabriqué sous licence par :..................................................

............................................................................................

Titre :..................................................................................

Date : ...................... Lieu : ...................... Dim. : ..............

en foi de quoi - pour que ceux qui ont des yeux voient -

j'autentifie :

............................................................................................

**(Daniel Spoerri)**

DANIEL SPOERRI, **Brevet de Garantie**, 1962

*"ready mades", "found objects", junk, records. This edition will sell for $ 8.00 to $ 10.00, depending on the quantity of nonreproducible matter or solids.*

Excerpt from Fluxus News-Policy-Letter No. 1, May 21, 1962.

In the end Maciunas only produced **Fluxus 1,** and that was not finished until 1964. **Flux Year Box 2** appeared in 1966 and **Fluxpack 3** in 1975. The Fluxus newspapers and other pamphlets started to be published in May 1963 with **Fluxus Preview Review**, and in January 1964 the first of the Fluxus newspapers, **Fluxus cc V TRE Fluxus**, appeared. Significantly, Maciunas expanded the idea of a collective anthology to many other formats: from **Fluxkit** (beginning in 1964–1965), to **Fluxfilms** (beginning in 1966), **Flux Post Kit 7** (1968), **Flux Toilet** (variations between 1968–1977), **Fluxlabyrinth** (1976), and to **Flux Cabinet** (1977).

Fluxus products were defined by George Maciunas. They were the logical development in the evolution of his thinking about the Fluxus movement, and existed concurrently with the other aspects of the movement, at times overlapping, at times contradicting, even sometimes intertwined with Fluxus events. Works would occur as a result of performance activities, or as elements of participation environments, as ideas for altered foods or for furniture. Maciunas' mind was open to all sorts of possibilities. From the smallest of stimuli he was able to develop numerous ideas. Some Fluxus works have a similar outward appearance, because he would specify a particular format or use. For example, in

1964 when he sent out small plastic boxes to artists and invited them to suggest ideas to fit, the result was a similarity of packaging in a number of Fluxus editions produced during that period.

With a few exceptions, George Maciunas himself drew up every individual Fluxus edition and the collective Fluxus anthologies. An artist would give him the idea, such as George Brecht's **Valoche** – French slang for traveling case. Brecht had made a unique version in 1959 called **The Case**. Taking the idea in the early 70's, Maciunas started producing a Fluxus edition using an 18-compartment plastic storage box with a label he had designed for Brecht's **Games & Puzzles** series. Brecht reacted to this assembly by suggesting that Maciunas use old wooden cases, and that he "stay away from plastic" in the selection of objects the box contained. Maciunas changed the label and contents so that in a late version of the work in 1978 it contained toys, balls, furry things, a blown egg, a fishing bobber and so on, things that one might take on a journey back to childhood. Maciunas was obsessed with this piece in the last months of his life, and spent hours carefully choosing objects and antique boxes to put things in, then pasting down labels he had designed for the work. Finally, not being able to affix the labels, he would lay them on top of the objects, but he would never let others choose what would go into a particular box. It was as though he were packing travelling kits with the things he would need most in the next world.

Sometimes he would pick up an idea from one of the Fluxus artists during a casual conversation and some years later produce an edition of the work. This happened with Robert Filliou's **Fluxdust** – nicely packaged floor sweepings brought out in 1966. In a discussion with Filliou he told me "two other projects were realized by George Maciunas. They came like this, in a conversation, probably over a beer in London when we met at the **Festival of Misfits**, and I mentioned having a collection of hair and dust. I then tought no more about it. By the time it was published, I had totally forgotten the idea".

A few Fluxus works were actually mass-produced, if 500 can be called mass production, but usually each work was carefully assembled by Maciunas, who would vary the contents as elements ran out or as his attitude towards the work changed.

No Fluxfactory was ever built. His spartan apartment was the sweat-shop where the assembly line for the "mass production" vied for space with projects as diverse as the design for issues of **Film Culture**, flyers for Christo's show at the Leo Castelli gallery or his endless attempts to chart the development and flow of art history, migrations, and learning.

On his return to Europe in the Fall of 1961, he continued to work on elements to be printed and inserted into La Monte Young's **An Anthology**. Such inserts were to form a major design element in **Fluxus I** and, by extension, individual Fluxus items. During the winter and spring of 1961–1962 Maciunas was working intently on plans for the various issues of **Fluxus Yearboxes** and a planned month-long festival of new music. Ultimately, production of **Fluxus I** took almost 3 years. **Japanese Fluxus**, **East European** and **French Fluxus**, and several other planned yearboxes were never published as such.

By the end of July 1962 he had already produced one-day Fluxus events in Wuppertal, Düsseldorf, and Paris, and was planning the month-long **Festum Fluxorum** in Wiesbaden, Germany for September 1962. During this period he was corresponding with Robert Watts and others urging them to send material for the regular and "luxus" issues of the yearboxes. The "luxus" issues were to include "inserts, records, moulded sheets, originals", etc., many of the type of things that would later go into **Fluxkits** and individual Fluxus editions.

In October 1962 Maciunas wrote to La Monte Young lamenting the control that Editions Peters, the music publishers, had over John Cage's works: "There is no way of reprinting it, since Peters owns Cage completely... We can't even perform Cage without paying some fee to GEMA... All very commercial...". The comment is ironic in the light of a series of letters he would write to artists barely a month later, requesting that they give him exclusive rights to publish their works in the name of Fluxus.

> *"... Would you care to have all your past & future works published under one cover or in box – a kind of special fluxus editon. this could be sold separately or as part of fluxus yearbox. I am going to publish such special Fluxus editions containing <u>complete</u> works of: George Brecht, Ben Patterson, Emmett Williams, Tomas Schmit, Nam June Paik (maybe), Henry Flynt, Robert Filliou, La Monte Young. This project – if continued could result in a nice & extensive liberary – or "encyclopedia" of good works being done these days. A kind of Shosoin warehouse of today. <u>One</u> condition however. I will finance & distribute these books, boxes, supply you with a few 100's, for your own $, BUT I <u>must</u> have exclusive right to publish them AND ALL YOUR FUTURE WORKS. A kind Faust – Mefisto, Cage – Peters deal. All works will be copy-righted (internationally) so no copies will be permitted & no performances without some $ to you ..."*

Letter: George Maciunas to Robert Watts (probably December 1962)

It is possible that Maciunas had offered an exclusive "publishing agreement" to more than twenty artists. Although some went along with his scheme, or vision, many, like La Monte Young, did not and distanced themselves from Fluxus.

Rapidly the emphasis of Fluxus publications grew from the numerous proposed **Fluxus Yearboxes** and collected works by individual artists to the idea of expanded kits containing all sorts of works by individuals, and collective kits with works by many artists. One of the letters Maciunas wrote to Robert Watts exploring these possibilities is a vivid example of the imagination and humor the two artists shared:

> *"... we could publish 100 boxes – each containing objects which you would 'mass-produce' like in a factory – pencils that don't write, leaking ink bottles, etc. Lollipops chrome plated – all wonderful stuff – NO PHOTOGRAPHS, – BUT OBJECTS – Like a suitcase of goodies.*

*Then why flatten out people – easier to flatten out animals like frogs. Catch 100 frogs put in press – & we put in book. Or maybe can get people from morgue – flatten (they will increase in size very much, so then they either must be cut to 100 pages or folded like newspaper). So I suggest for box to do like this: Like a travelers suitcase a 'travelers kit', sell for maybe $ 50 or so. Then inside all compartmentalized … the suitcase can be sold as a whole or only parts of – each compartment separately. We can advertise say in New Yorker & say for $ 50 this 'hand crafted attache case with all that a businessman – traveler needs' – & maybe sell 100 of them, then we make another 100 or start a factory!!? … Those Yam lectures – things – I am very interested. But I think we should have a COMMON FRONT – CENTRALIZATION of all such activities. Yam there, Fluxus here. – not so good, why not combine all into one effort – So we can make world Revolution with Yamflux??? … So I think all PROLETARIANS SHOULD UNITE!!! COMMON FRONT!!! … My efforts now are to enlist good people … from Japan & East Europe … But it needs propaganda effort. That's why we push so hard with Fluxus festivals, so we start catching good fish … Next weekend I will go to Wuppertal where Paik is completing setting up his 'exhibit' and make a very detailed photo – reportage of his TV sets, pianos, etc. etc. …"*

Letter: George Maciunas to Robert Watts [before March 11, 1963]

George Maciunas designed and produced the Fluxus edition of Robert Watts' **Events** in 1964. This work was continuously available from Fluxus well into the 1970s, the contents and packaging changing over the years. Fluxus also produced or distributed perhaps 100 other works by Robert Watts, although it never had an "exclusive right" to all his works.

At the same time that Maciunas was writing to Robert Watts about the prospect of producing a "traveler's kit" of his works, he was setting up the first Fluxus exhibition. It was a small show of objects and instructions by George Brecht, Tomas Schmit, Watts, and Ben Vautier in the kitchen of the Galerie Parnass in Wuppertal, where Nam June Paik was holding his first exhibition of altered TV sets and prepared pianos. Exhibits of Fluxus works over the years were to serve the practical function of promoting Fluxus and distributing the works. Sometimes Maciunas would come up with special ideas for their display, such as standard cubes that could hold different items. Although works would be handled during exhibits, the primary purpose was to sell the objects and promote Fluxus.

**Fluxus Preview Review** appeared in May or June 1963 and was the first publication about Fluxus' plans since the two "Brochure Prospectuses" were distributed in June and September 1962, and the **Fluxus Manifesto** was thrown at the audience in Düsseldorf in February 1963. The optimistic list of Fluxus works being offered for sale included 9 yearboxes to be produced in the next two years, including a **Luxus Fluxus US yearbox with tapes, film loops, objects, originals, each edition different** for $ 12, and a $ 10 **French Yearbox** luxus edition with tape, Spoerri's **L'Optique Moderne** and the complete works of Robert Filliou. The list of **Fluxus Special Editions 1963–1964** included Paik's **Monthly Review of the University of Avant-Garde Hinduism** for "$ 8 per year" plus **the smallest book of the world, largest book of the world**, etc. Works which did appear, like the Spoerri book, included Brecht's **Water Yam** and La Monte Young's **Compositions 1961**. Among works that did not appear as Fluxus editions were: Emmett Williams' **Complete Works**, Robert Filliou's **Complete Works**, Ben Patterson's **Complete Works**, Tomas Schmit's **Complete Works**, Henry Flynt's **Expandable Box**, La Monte Young's **Complete Works**, Ben Vautier's **Complete Works**, and Toshi Ichiyanagi's **Complete Works**. Yoko Ono's **Complete Works** were self-published in Japan the following year as **Grapefruit**, and Allan Kaprow's **Paintings, Environments & Happenings** was eventually published by Harry N. Abrams several years later, with the title **Assemblages, Environments and Happenings**. Scores by special order of Ichiyanagi, Matsudaira, Tone, Yuasa, Schnebel and others were also offered. Many of these were produced by Fluxus using a method developed by C.F. Peters, which published copies of scores on demand, printing them with an ozalid or blueprint process from a master original. Maciunas' approach to Fluxus production took on Vaudeville qualities as this late spring 1963 letter to Ben Vautier suggests.

*"... In regards to Fluxus copyrights etc. on your works. I think no one will object to your special publication of 100 copies of some works. In fact you could note that they are Fluxus SSS or SSSS or SSSSS publications. Assuming we asign letter 'S' to all your works publications etc. For instance Nam June Paik has 'g' for his first publication, then 'gg' for 2nd, ggg for 3rd, gggg, ggggg, ggg – etc – Under same system you could send out original text, objects to limited mailing list. You could choose various letter combinations starting with S – ad infinitum. Say – 1st mailing to be Fluxus SMXOV then SVOMX etc., etc. infinite number of combinations. Anything starting with S (or any other letter, maybe you prefer 'V'?) would indicate as your Fluxus number (or rather letter) ..."*
Letter: George Maciunas to Ben Vautier, late May/early June 1963

In the fall of 1963 Maciunas returned to New York and moved into a loft on Canal Street, an area filled with job-lot shops, merchandizers of cheap plastic boxes, electrical bits and pieces, which quickly began to be included in Fluxus Editions.

An announcement in the first issue of the Fluxus newspaper **Fluxus cc V TRE Fluxus** January 1964, listed the Fluxus editions of 1963 available for sale ranging from La Monte Young's **Compositions 1961** in paper covers at $ 1 to Chieko Shiomi's **Endless Box** at $ 20. Editions planned for 1964 were still modest, but included Robert Watts' **Suitcase** at $ 40. At the end of the list of works for sale, Maciunas put this notice:

*Most materials originally intended for Fluxus yearboxes will be included in the FLUXUSccV TRE newspaper or in individual boxes.*

Underlying his activities was a fundamental, revolutionary attitude in favor of the "collective spirit". He saw Fluxus as being "against (the) art-object as (a) non-functional commodity", and closer in attitude to the NOVYI LEF (Novyi Levyi Front Iskusstv – New Left Front of the Arts) group of the late 1920s in the

Soviet Union. Being able to live and produce works as cheaply as possible was a preoccupation of his. He devised elaborate schemes for utilizing materials. Labels from food containers found their way into some of John Chick's **Flux Food** boxes, or were used for Maciunas' own **One Year**. His medicine bottles were recycled into several other works: Shigeko Kubota's **Flux Medicine**, Carla Liss' **Sacrament Fluxkit**, Geoffrey Hendricks' **Flux Reliquary**, Mieko Shiomi's **Water Music**, Ben Vautier's **Dirty Water**, and Ken Friedman's **Cleanliness FluxKit**. When Maciunas produced an edition of George Brecht and Robert Filliou's **Eastern Daylight Flux Time** using the cases of cheap pocket watches, he would utilize the mechanisms from inside the watches for Robert Watts' **Flux Timekit**.

Although he complained of "very little enthusiasm here..." in New York, between January and June 1964 he produced four **Fluxus** newspapers, a series of Fluxus concerts in the **Fluxhall** (his Canal Street loft) and on the streets nearby, the **Fluxus Symphony Orchestra Concert** at Carnegie Recital Hall, a number of Fluxus editions, and picketed Stockhausen's concert with the **Action Against Cultural Imperialism** group. The March newspaper advertised numerous works including some by George Brecht taken over from the list in the Yam newspaper, such as a **No Smoking** sign. Other works included **Bolts** and **House Numbers** – existing works given over to Fluxus which were easily producible and in keeping with a Duchampian aesthetic of the ready-made. By June 1964, Maciunas was writing to Willem de Ridder and others describing collective anthologies called **Flux-kits (suitcases)** which he was assembling.

Using an idea from Marcel Duchamp, **Fluxkits** are altered attaché cases modified to fit a whole selection of Fluxus editions and publications by many artists. Their contents changed from case to case as new works were produced. Maciunas saw them as portable Fluxus Museums – the sample cases of the traveling salesmen of Fluxus. The contents of the earliest **Fluxkit** differed from the 25 to 30 later examples, in that several of the labels, scores, instructions, and photographs had not yet been printed, and he used original or hand-made material for those works instead. In fact, many works in all **Fluxkits** were hand-assembled, from Mieko Shiomi's **Endless Box**, which she constructed herself, to the collage elements in Shigeko Kubota's **Flux Napkins**. Maciunas would carefully weigh and mark each pebble in Robert Watts' **Rocks Marked by Weight in Grams** sometimes painting the numbers on, sometimes using "handprinting" or a protective medium.

Willem de Ridder had use of a space at Amstel 47 in Amsterdam where he showed Nam June Paik's **Piano for all Senses** in June and July of 1963. These prepared pianos were "interpreted and realized" by Tomas Schmit, Manfred Montwé, Peter Brötzmann, and de Ridder. Well into 1964 he continued to produce events and show art works in that space as well as selling various Fluxus works that Maciunas sent to him. During the spring of 1964, de Ridder published the first of two pricelists of his **European Mail-Order Warehouse Fluxshop**, based on lists Maciunas published in the **Fluxus** newspapers.

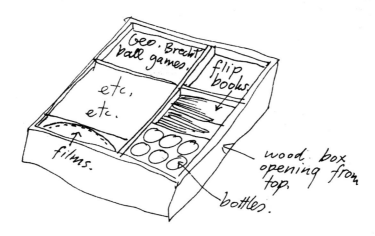

GEORGE MACIUNAS Design für **Flux Year Box 2,** 1965

By March 1965 the fifth **Fluxus** newspaper was offering more than 200 different works for sale. However, most still only existed as ideas or prototypes, and were often made only on request. Some, on the other hand, such as works by George Brecht and Arthur Koepcke, already existed and were put on the list of Fluxus works. Distribution of Fluxus products was advertised as being through **Fluxshops** and by mail order. These outlets were:

FLUX – HQ
MAILORDERS, FACTORY, WAREHOUSE, FLUXFESTS
P.O.BOX 180, CANAL ST.STA. NEW YORK, NY. 10013

FLUXSHOP & FLUXFESTS – NEW YORK
CINEMATHEQUE

FLUXSHOP & FLUXFESTS – EUROPE NORTH
WILLEM DE RIDDER, POSTBOX 2045  AMSTERDAM
HOLLAND

FLUXSHOP & FLUXFESTS – EUROPE SOUTH
BEN VAUTIER, 32 RUE TONDUTTI DE L'ESCARENE
NICE, FRANCE

FLUXSHOP JAPAN (PROVISIONAL)
c/o KUNIHARU AKIYAMA, 3-814 MATSUBARACHO,
SETAGAYAKU, TOKYO, JAPAN.

It was a good front, though most were merely shelves stacked with materials that Maciunas provided. Ben Vautier, however, did have a real shop, a wonderful recordshop where all sorts of activities took place. The most ambitious of the satellite **Fluxshops** was certainly in Amsterdam. In order to promote the **European Mail-Order Warehouse/Fluxshop**, Willem de Ridder set up a mass of Fluxus editions and publications on the couch in the living room of his home in Amsterdam. His friend Dorothea Meijer, who was helping de Ridder with the administration of the Fluxus shop and other projects, posed provocatively in the midst of all the works. A series of photographs was taken, and the display was dismantled. That evening de Ridder made an erotic film on the same couch.

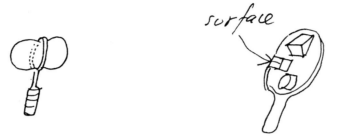

In addition elements of **Fluxus Games** began to take on the character of Fluxus objects. George Maciunas would make holes in ping-pong rackets, or hide lead under the rubber on paddles, making them very heavy. There was a variety of altered shoes, including shoes with spikes on the soles, and many more sports-related altered objects. The press release for the **Flux Orchestra at Carnegie Recital Hall**, September 1965 in New York, gives a good sense of the direction Fluxus production was now taking:

> "… *An exhibit of various Fluxus mass produced products and publications will be presented by Fluxshop at the Carnegie Recital Reception Room. It will consist of the following: Fluxyearboxes, Fluxus newspapers, Fluxkit (containing entire set of Fluxus publications). Fluxchess and Musical chairs by Takako Saito, Finger hole set by Ayo, Games and Puzzles by George Brecht and Robert Watts, Fluxmusicmachine by Joe Jones, Fluxorgan, Fluxtablecloths by Daniel Spoerri, Fluxclothing by Robert Watts, Spatial Poem by Chieko Shiomi, Touch poems by Yoko Ono, Peep show box by Anthony Cox, Fluxfilms (which can be viewed by eye viewers). These products will be offered for sale.*"

Within a few months Maciunas was to produce the first version of **Fluxfilms**. The anthology of Fluxus films is another example of his desire to produce collective projects and works that could be distributed to promote the movement. The first anthology, which was produced in 1966, contains works by Yoko Ono, Joe Jones, George Maciunas, Paul Sharits, Wolf Vostell, Robert Watts and others. They are innovative films exploring the possibilities of the medium rather than telling a story or documenting an event. Yoko Ono's **Film No. 4** is a close-up sequence of naked bottoms walking, Jim Riddle's **9 Minutes** is 9 minutes of film ticking off time, Chieko Shiomi's **Disappearing Music for Face** is a smile, shot with a high-speed camera, then projected at normal speed. The **Fluxfilms** are also an example of how one project could be used for many different purposes. Besides the long and short versions of **Fluxfilms**, in 8 mm and 16 mm, the films were used in 8 mm looped versions in **Flux Year Box 2** and in a separate Fluxus

WILLEM DE RIDDER **European Mail-Order House/Fluxshop (1964-1965)**
(Photo Wim van der Linden)

GEORGE MACIUNAS
Label for **Fluxfilms**, ca. 1966 (see 131 d)

edition packaging. 16 mm loops of Paik's **Zen for Film** and Higgins' **Invocation of Canyons and Boulders** were also produced as separate Fluxus edition boxes. Then loops of the films were projected round the walls of a room like wallpaper. A 3' x 3' x 3' suspended booth described as a "capsule" was also planned for projections. Wallpaper of Yoko Ono's **Film No. 4** was produced by Maciunas who attributed it to Vautier. Other printed wallpapers from film images were planned. Flipbooks of Shiomi's **Disappearing Music for Face** and Higgins' **Invocation of Canyons and Boulders** were also produced.

Maciunas' interaction with certain Fluxus artists during this intense period of producing Fluxus editions is evident in a letter that he wrote to Ben Vautier on August 7, 1966. I will quote extensively from this letter in order to show the variety of works that Maciunas was producing for Fluxus, and to demonstrate one of the processes in the development of Fluxus works. Here Vautier had asked several artists with whom he was associated in Nice to contribute ideas for Maciunas and Fluxus.

*"... Now I can reply to your letter with suggestions for various Flux items. THEY ARE ALL GREAT!!! I will print labels for them all. False Flux box by Ben; Flux clock (2 clocks, one right, one defective) by Ben; Flux shop locations (atlas) by Ben; Flux useless objects, maybe should be called Flux-sample? by Ben; Flux dots; Flux contents, maybe call Fluxdrink? or Fluxwine, by Serge Oldenbourg – (plaster in bottle). I like his idea, very nice & easy to produce; Flux art collections, by Allocco; Flux light by Ben (could have many variations, like a 8 volt light with 115 volt cord, so it would burn out as soon as you switched it on); Flux egg (maybe to fragile); Flux mobile – (seeds) VERY GOOD! By Ben or Annie?; Fluxcertificates, OK! by Ben;*

*Fluxanything box, by Ben; Fluxnothing ' '(by Ben); Fluxpainting ' '(by Ben); Flux mystery food! (by Ben) VERY GOOD & easy to produce using readymade cans. OK; Fluxsuicide Kit by Ben; Fluxcatalog, by Ben (dictionary) OK!!; Flux missing card set VERY GOOD & easy!!; Fluxcolors OK!; Fluxdeclarations ...*

*Another new development: We are working on FLUXFURNITURE. Peter Moore: Venetian blinds; you pull one way – girl all dressed (full size photo) pull another way – girl nude. Rug – nude girl all spread out (photo reproduction) like a bear rug; Tables: Laminated full size photos (Spoerri's 35 variations) Bob Watts – a disorderly desk (all photographic). or one top with full size photo of girls crossed legs, so when you sit on correct side it looks as if these legs belong to you. very funny effect. Then many chairs and cabinets with various kinds of doors. 15" x 15" One has 25 clock faces printed, but one has real clock arms moving, although from distance they all look alike. Another is like medicine cabinet, 1st door has photo of squeezed front face. 2nd door has photo dish (like radar screen) so you see 50 faces of yourself. etc. etc.*

*N.Y. Times photographed them all for a special Furniture feature for September Sunday magazine should give us finally our 1st publicity here. If you like, think up new furniture ideas, and I will manufacture them, I will also ship some of them to you as soon as I have some money ..."*

In the **Fluxus Newsletter** of March 8, 1967, Maciunas announced the formation of **Implosions Inc.** and a project called **Fluxhouse Cooperative Building Project** to buy and renovate loft buildings in SOHO for artists. Started way before its time, but when the market for trivia was booming in the 60s, **Implosions Inc.** was on the one hand a device to market Fluxus and Fluxus-like items profitably. On the other hand, it was an attempt to find a way to mass-produce and distribute Fluxus materials once he realized that the distribution systems he had established were not working, and were in effect imitating structures he was trying to combat. **Implosions**, however, was also a failure.

   **Fluxhouse Cooperatives** were designed to give artists affordable, legal possession of their living and working spaces. Maciunas' work in this area led directly to the creation of SOHO as an artists' district in New York. He was to devote enormous energy to the purchase and renovation of loft buildings until the time of his death, gaining nothing personally from this exercise.

*FLUXNEWSLETTER, DECEMBER 2, 1968*

*...*

*FLUX-CHRISTMAS MEAL EVENT*
*all are invited to participate by bringing a prepared meal or drink event. Notify me in advance what you will prepare. See last newsletter for examples.*

*...*

*FLUXSHOP*
*At 16 Greene st. 2nd floor 16' x 85' space. Similar arrangement as per enclosed proposal for gallery 669 (never realized), with addition of:*
*a) time punch clock, printing on visitors cards anything but time (suggestions from all will be welcome)*

*b) cash register, each key (total 36) mechanically or electrically connected to activate some action or event. (snowfall, lights off, loud sound, blast of spice, other smells, trap door, etc. suggestions welcome).*

*...*

*PROPOSALS WILL BE WELCOME FOR:*
  *1. radio-TV pieces*
  *2. biographies*
  *3. sport game events for fluxolympiad, new games for Flux-year-box 3.*
  *4. new pieces for the Fluxorchestra*
  *5. new films and film loops for film environment*
  *6. any other new pieces for the Fluxfest*
  *7. new ideas for clock faces*
  *8. new ideas for aprons and stick-ons*
  *9. new toilet room objects*
  *10. meal or drink for christmas party (place & time to be announced)*
  *11. time punch clock dies (for printing on cards)*
  *12. cash register key events*

*PROPOSED FLUXSHOW FOR GALLERY 669, LOS ANGELES. OPENING NOV. 26, 1968*
  *1. STREET EVENTS ...*
  *2. VESTIBULE VARIATIONS, by Ayo ...*
  *3. FOOD CENTER ...*
  *4. SPORTS-GAME CENTER ...*
  *5. CLINIC by Hi Red Center ...*
  *6. AUTOMATIC VENDING MACHINES – DISPENSERS (coin operated) ...*
  *7. FILM WALLPAPER ENVIRONMENT ...*
  *8. SOUND ENVIRONMENT (may be within film environment) ...*
  *9. SOUND MACHINES ...*
  *10. OBJECTS, FURNITURE ...*
  *11. WALL OF POSTERS, PAST NEWSPAPERS (V TRE), (one of a kind) ...*
  *12. TOILET OBJECTS ...*

Fluxnewsletter, December 2, 1968 [Excerpts]

By the end of 1968, as these excerpts from the **Fluxus Newsletter** show, Maciunas had expanded the ideas of Fluxus objects in many directions, enlarging the scope of a Fluxus work to include environments, meals, game centers, vending machine arcades, furniture, sound machines, etc., always requesting suggestions and ideas from artists associated with the Fluxus movement. He was fascinated with the possibilites of altering the functions of toilets. After the plans for a **FluxToilet** at the 1970 **Happening & Fluxus** show in Cologne became entangled in red tape, Maciunas pursued other possibilities, distributing a plan for a collective **FluxToilet** in an April 1973 **Fluxus Newsletter**. Several of the toilet variations were realized during the **Fluxfest** and/or at an alternative art space in Seattle, Washington in 1977.

*PRELIMINARY PROPOSAL FOR A FLUX EXHIBIT AT RENE BLOCK*
*GALLERY, 409 WEST BROADWAY*

*...*

*FLUX AMUSEMENT ARCADE*
1. *Vending machines, dispensers of holy relics (Hendricks), endless string, prepared eggs, drinks before cups etc. (Maciunas)*
2. *Stamp & postcard dispensers (Watts & Vautier)*
3. *Ticket dispenser (tickets by John Lennon, Vautier, Ayo, Maciunas, Wada)*
4. *Weighing scale (Watts), Pin-ball game (Maciunas), movie-loop machine (flux-films from Flux-box 2), target*
5. *Bill Tarr's closet for people (being inundated in ping-pong balls) 3 x 3 x 6 ft high*
6. *Ben Vautier's suicide booth, 3 x 6 x 6 ft high*
7. *Nam June Paik's prepared piano*
8. *Clinic & test booth (Hi Red Center, Watts, Maciunas, etc.) 6 x 6 x 6 ft cubicle (need one or two full-time attendants, I could supply)*
9. *Joe Jones automatic trio with Maciunas aerophone (coin activated)*
10. *Ayo's floor obstacles (either in staircase or a maze (12 x 12 x 6 ft high cubicle)*
11. *cabinets, chests and trunks with collection of past & current flux-boxes, objects (have about 8 antique cabinets for such a purpose)*
12. *Flux toilet (3 prepared toilets will be constructed at 80 Wooster St. basement, could be completed by December)*

*FLUX GAME ROOM*
1. *Swing tournament (Maciunas)*
2. *Floor billiard with paper boxes (Takako Saito)*
3. *Prepared ping-pong (Maciunas)*
4. *Hot cockles (Robin Crozier)*

*...*

*Vending machines and flux-objects could be sold; but everything else would be of no monetary value.*
*Furthermore you would have to carry some sort of insurance to cover damage of objects and constructions ...*

Preliminary Proposal for a Flux Exhibit at René Block Gallery, 409 West Broadway **Fluxus Newsletter** by George Maciunas, New York ca. 1974. Excerpts.

Maciunas had many ideas for **Fluxus Game Centers** which he viewed as expanded anthologies of Fluxus amusements. Aspects of these ideas often appeared in **Fluxfests**, although he was never able to establish a permanent **Game Center.** The **Fluxlabyrinth** in Berlin in September 1976 did succeed in being a sustained environmental structure with a variety of activities designed by several Fluxus artists.

The last collective Fluxus anthology that Maciunas constructed was the **Flux Cabinet** in 1977. The work contains games and mysteries, and also a labyrinth where the balls fall through to the drawers below. There is a pop-up rubber glass that doesn't pop-up, a work attributed to two artists, and of course his own **Excreta Fluxorum**, a marvelous shit anthology. Had he lived, Maciunas would certainly have gone on producing more Fluxus editions and collective anthologies, for he saw them as an integral part of Fluxus.

Arriving at a functional definition of a Fluxus work is really quite straightforward. It's not to do with aesthetics, a recognizable style, size or medium. Rather it is to do with a certain willingness on the part of an artist to throw an idea or work into a pot stirred and seasoned by George Maciunas, and to let it exist concurrently with other works by artists in the group, at times mutating and metamorphosing. There are a few generally applicable terms such as "cheap", "mass-producible", "disposable", "funny", "gag-like", "ready-made", etc. However, Fluxus works form an enormous corpus that is rich in variety and intentionally defies generalization.

Quite simply, a Fluxus work is one that was given to Maciunas to distribute, or an idea produced as a Fluxus edition, or devised by Maciunas, and listed or advertised in one of the Fluxus publications, newsletters, handbills, or flyers, or discussed in correspondence with Maciunas, who agreed to produce the work. Additional Fluxus works are altered ready-made elements of Fluxus environments, Fluxus sports events, Fluxus feasts, and Fluxus performances, or objects specially constructed for those activities.

Perhaps his intentions for Fluxus and Fluxus products can best be summarized by the 1965 manifesto, where he compares "art" to "Fluxus Art-Amusement":

*ART*
*To justify artist's professional, parasitic and elite status in society,*
*he must demonstrate artist's indispensability and exclusiveness,*
*he must demonstrate the dependability of audience upon him,*
*he must demonstrate that no one but the artist can do art.*

*Therefore, art must appear to be complex, pretentious, profound, serious, intellectual, inspired, skillfull, significant, theatrical, it must appear to be valuable as commodity so as to provide the artist with an income.*
*To raise its value (artist's income and patrons profit), art is made to appear rare, limited in quantity and therefore obtainable and accessible only to the social elite and institutions.*

*FLUXUS ART-AMUSEMENT*
*To establish artist's nonprofessional status in society,*
*he must demonstrate artist's dispensability and inclusiveness,*
*he must demonstrate the selfsufficiency of the audience,*
*he must demonstrate that anything can be art and anyone can do it.*

*Therefore, art-amusement must be simple, amusing, unpretentious, concerned with insignificances, require no skill or countless rehearsals, have no commodity or institutional value.*
*The value of art-amusement must be lowered by making it unlimited, massproduced, obtainable by all and eventually produced by all.*

*Fluxus art-amusement is the rear-guard without any pretention or urge to participate in the competition of "one-upmanship" with the avant-garde. It strives for the monostructural and nontheatrical qualities of simple natural event, a game or a gag. It is the fusion of Spikes Jones, Vaudeville, gag, children's games and Duchamp.*

Fluxus Broadside Manifest. [New York, ca. September, 1965] Excerpt


George Maciunas was a complex genius, driven by a utopian vision of a new art and a new society. He saw Fluxus as both an amusement and a device to undermine the preciousness of art. He valued Functionalism, but never indulged in futility. A metaphor for Maciunas' sense of the Fluxus paradigm might be Robert Filliou's **Futile Box** – a planned Fluxus edition that was never produced by Fluxus. The box had hinged doors opening at both the top and bottom, and contained a ball which was larger than the box. When the lid was closed, the bottom hatch opened and the ball fell out, etc.

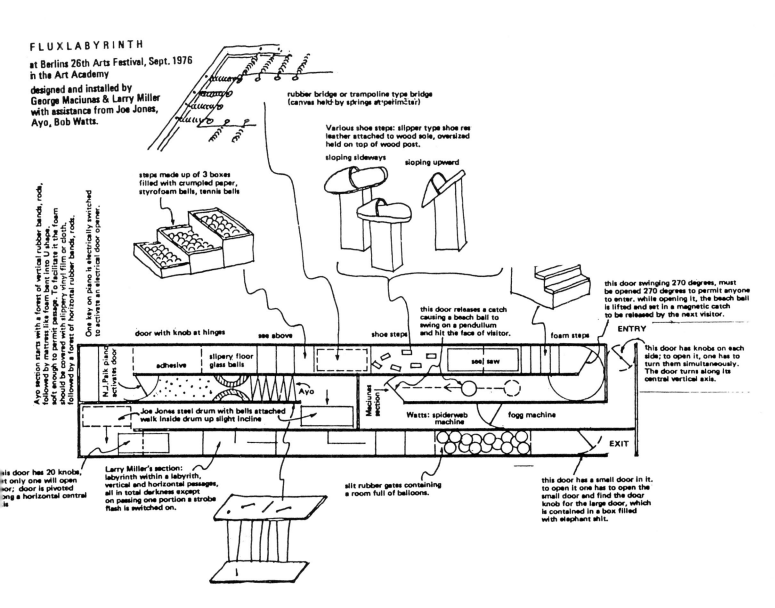

# FLUXLABYRINTH

**at Berlins 26th Arts Festival, Sept. 1976 in the Art Academy**

designed and installed by
**George Maciunas & Larry Miller**
with assistance from Joe Jones,
Ayo, Bob Watts.

rubber bridge or trampoline type bridge
(canvas held by springs at perimeter)

Various shoe steps: slipper type shoe res
leather attached to wood sole, oversized
held on top of wood post.

sloping sideways        sloping upward

steps made up of 3 boxes
filled with crumpled paper,
styrofoam balls, tennis balls

Ayo section starts with a forest of vertical rubber bands, rods,
followed by mattress like foam bent into U shape,
soft enough to permit passage. To facilitate it the foam
should be covered with slippery vinyl film or cloth,
followed by a forest of horizontal rubber bands, rods.

One key on piano is electrically switched
to activate an electrical door opener.

this door swinging 270 degrees, must
be opened 270 degrees to permit anyone
to enter. while opening it, the beach ball
is lifted and set in a magnetic catch
to be released by the next visitor.

this door releases a catch
causing a beach ball to
swing on a pendulum
and hit the face of visitor.

**ENTRY**

door with knob at hinges    see above    shoe steps    foam steps

this door has knobs on each
side; to open it, one has to
turn them simultaneously.
The door turns along its
central vertical axis.

N.J.Paik piano
activates door    adhesive    slippery floor    see saw
                              glass balls

Ayo

Maciunas
section

Watts: spiderweb    fogg machine
machine

Joe Jones steel drum with bells attached
walk inside drum up slight incline

**EXIT**

is door has 20 knobs,
t only one will open
or; door is pivoted
ong a horizontal central
is

Larry Miller's section:
labyrinth within a labyrinth,
vertical and horizontal passages,
all in total darkness except
on passing one portion a strobe
flash is switched on.

slit rubber gates containing
a room full of balloons.

this door has a small door in it.
to open it one has to open the
small door and find the door
knob for the large door, which
is contained in a box filled
with elephant shit.

GEORGE MACIUNAS

**luxlabyrinth at Berlin's 26th Arts Festival, September 1976**
istributed as **Fluxus Newsletter,** Fall 1976

## Selected Bibliography

- **Aktionen, Vernissagen, Personen: Die Rheinische Kunstszene der 50er und 60er Jahre. Eine Fotodokumentation von Manfred Leve.** exh. cat. Köln: Rheinland-Verlag, 1982

- Alocco. Marcel, et. al. **Fluxus à Nice.** Nice: Z'éditions, 1989

- Andersch, Erik, Andreas Beaugrand, and Friedemann Malsch, eds. **Fluxus aus der Sammlung Andersch.** exh. cat. Bielefeld: Kunsthalle, 1992

- Anderson, Simon. **Fluxus Early Years and Close Correspondences.** MA Thesis, n. d. (Archiv Sohm, Staatsgalerie Stuttgart)

- **AQ** 16 (1977). „How We Met: Or a Microdemystification"

- Armstrong, Elizabeth, and Joan Rothfuss. **In the Spirit of Fluxus.** exh. cat. Minneapolis: Walker Art Center, 1993

- **Art and Artists** Vol. 7, no. 7 (October 1972). „Free Fluxus Now"

- Auslander, Philip. **A History of Fluxus Performance.** MA Thesis, Hunter College, The City University of New York, 1980

- Baerwaldt Wayne, ed. **Under the Influence of Fluxus.** exh. cat. Winnipeg: Plug in Inc., 1992

- Becker, Jürgen, and Wolf Vostell. **Happenings, Fluxus, Pop Art, Nouveau Réalisme: Eine Dokumentation.** Hamburg: Rowohlt, 1965

- Block, René, ed. **1962 Wiesbaden Fluxus 1982: Eine kleine Geschichte von Fluxus in drei Teilen.** exh. cat. Wiesbaden: Harlekin Art and Berlin: Berliner Künstlerprogramm des DAAD, 1983

- ibid. „Fluxus and Fluxism in Berlin 1964–1976." In **Berlinart 1961–1987,** edited by Kynaston McShine, pp. 65–79. exh. cat. New York: Museum of Modern Art, 1987

- ibid., ed. **Fluxus Da Capo: 1962 Wiesbaden 1992.** exh. cat. Wiesbaden: Nassauischer Kunstverein, Kulturamt der Landeshauptstadt Wiesbaden, and Harlekin Art/Fluxeum, 1992

- Conzen-Meairs, Ina, ed. **Liber Maister S: Hanns Sohm zum siebzigsten Geburtstag.** Stuttgart: Staatsgalerie, 1991

- ibid. **George Maciunas.** Künstler. Kritisches Lexikon der Gegenwartskunst. Ausgabe 22. München: WB Verlag, 1993

- Di Maggio, Gino and Achille Bonito Oliva, eds. **Ubi Fluxus Ibi Motus 1990–1962.** exh. cat. Milano: Nuove Edizioni Gabriele Mazzotta, 1990.

- Dreyfus, Charles. **Fluxus/elements d'information.** exh. cat. Paris: Arc 2-Museé d'art moderne de la ville de Paris, 1974

- ibid. **Happenings & Fluxus.** exh. cat. Paris: Galerie du Génie and Galerie de Poche, 1989

- **Film Culture 43** (Winter 1966). "Expanded Arts Issue."

- **Fluxus: o del „principio d'indeterminazione."** exh. cat. Genova: Studio Leonardi-Unimedia, 1988

– **Fluxus S.P.Q.R.** exh. cat. Verona: Adriano Parise, 1990

– **Fluxus Virus 1962–1992.** exh. cat. Köln: Galerie Schüppenhauer and München: Aktionsforum Praterinsel, 1992

– **Flash Art.** no. 84–85 (October–November 1978)

– **Freibord: Zeitschrift für Literatur und Kunst** 60 (1987). „Fluxus–25 Years"

– **Freibord: Zeitschrift für Literatur und Kunst** 64 (February 1986)

– **Freibord: Zeitschrift für Literatur und Kunst** 73 (March 1990). „Fluxus"

– Friedman, Ken, Peter Frank, and Elizabeth Brown. **Young Fluxus.** exh. cat. New York: Committee for the Visual Arts and Artists Space, 1982

– Hansen, Al. **A Primer of Happenings & Time/Space Art.** New York: Something Else Press, 1965

– Haskell, Barbara. **BLAM! the Explosion of Pop, Minimalism and Performance 1958–1964.** exh. cat. New York: Whitney Museum of American Art, in Association with W. W. Norton & Company. 1984

– Hendricks, Jon ed. **Fluxus Etc. The Gilbert and Lila Silverman Fluxus Collection.** exh. cat. Bloomfield Hills, Mich.: Cranbrook Academy of Art Museum, 1981

– ibid., ed. **Fluxus Etc./addenda I the Gilbert and Lila Silverman Fluxus Collection.** New York: Ink &, 1983

– ibid., ed. **Fluxus Etc./addenda II the Gilbert and Lila Silverman Fluxus Collection.** exh. cat. Pasadena: Baxter Art Gallery, 1983

– ibid., **Fluxus Codex.** With an introduction by Robert Pincus-Witten. The Gilbert and Lila Silverman Fluxus Collection, Detroit, Michigan, New York: Harry N. Abrams, Inc., 1988

– ibid. „Fluxus: Kleines Sommerfest / Neo-Dada in der Musik / Fluxus Internationale Festspiele Neuster Musik / Festum Fluxorum Fluxus, Wuppertal, Wiesbaden, Düsseldorf 1962/63." In **Stationen der Moderne. Die Bedeutenden Kunstaustellungen des 20. Jahrhunderts in Deutschland**, Eds. Michael Bolle and Eva Zuchner, pp. 492–517. exh. cat. Berlin: Berlinische Galerie, 1988

– Hendricks, Jon, and Clive Phillpot. **FLUXUS. Selections from the Gilbert and Lila Silverman Collection.** exh. cat. New York: Museum of Modern Art, 1988

– Herzogenrath, Wulf, and Gabriele Lueg, eds. **Die 60er Jahre. Kölns Weg zur Kunstmetropole. Vom Happening zum Kunstmarkt.** Köln: Kölnischer Kunstverein, 1986

– Higgins, Dick. **Jefferson's Birthday/Postface.** New York: Something Else Press, 1964

– ibid., ed. **Fluxus 25 Years.** exh. cat. Williamstown, Mass: Williams College Museum of Art, 1988

– Kellein, Thomas. „Fluxus – Eine Internationale des künstlerischen Mißlingens," pp. 325–336. In **Europa/Amerika. Die Geschichte einer künstlerischen Faszination seit 1940.** Eds. Gohr, Siegfried, and Rafael Jablonka. exh. cat. Köln: Museum Ludwig, 1986.

– ibid. **Fröhliche Wissenschaft. Das Archiv Sohm.** Stuttgart: Staatsgalerie, 1986

– Krinzinger, Ursula, ed. **Fluxus Subjektiv.** exh. cat. Wien: Galerie Krinzinger, 1990

– **Kunstforum International** 115 (September–Oktober 1991). „Fluxus – Ein Nachruf zu Lebzeiten"

– Lauf, Cornelia, and Susan Hapgood. eds. **FluxAttitudes.** exh. cat. Ghent. Imschoot Uitgevers. 1991

– **Lightworks** 11–12 (Fall 1979). „Fluxus"

– **Lund Art Press** 1, no. 4 (Summer–Autumn 1990)

– **Lund Art Press** 2, no. 2 (1991). „Fluxus Research"

– Martin, Henry. ed. **Fluxers.** exh. cat. Bozen/Bolzano: Museion, 1992

– Mayor, David, ed. **Fluxshoe.** exh. cat. Cullompton. Devon. England: Beau Geste Press, 1972

– Mayor, David, and Filipe Ehrenberg, eds. **Fluxshoe Add End A.** Cullompton, Devon, England: Beau Geste Press. 1973

– Milman, Estera. **Fluxus & Friends: Selections from the Alternative Traditions in the Contemporary Arts Collection.** exh. cat. Iowa City: University of Iowa Museum of Art, 1988

– Moore, Barbara. „George Maciunas: A Finger in Fluxus." **Artforum** 21, no. 2 (October 1982), pp. 38–45

– Moore, Peter. „Fluxus Focus". **Artforum** 21, no. 2 (October 1982). pp. 33–37

– Nannucci, Maurizio, ed. **Fluxus Anthology: A Collection of Music and Sound Events.** Long-playing record album. Florence: Zona Archives and Recordings, 1989

– **North** 15 (1985). „Fluxus: The Unpredictable Legend"

– Pedersen, Knud, and Ludwig Gosewitz. **Der Kampf gegen die Bürgermusik.** Köln: Michael Werner, 1973

– Peters, Ursula, and Georg F. Schwarzbauer, eds. **Fluxus – Aspekte eines Phänomens.** Wuppertal: Kunst- und Museumsverein Wuppertal, 1981

– Ruhé, Harry. **Fluxus, the most radical and experimental art movement of the sixties.** Amsterdam: „A", 1979

– Schilling, Jürgen. **Aktionskunst: Identität von Kunst und Leben?** Luzern und Frankfurt: J. C. Bucher, 1978

– Schwarz, Dieter. **Was ist Fluxus?** Winterthur: Kunstmuseum, 1991

– Smith, Owen F. **George Maciunas and a History of Fluxus; or, The Art Movement that Never Existed.** Diss. University of Washington, 1991

– Sohm, Hanns, and Harald Szeemann, eds. **happening & fluxus.** exh. cat. Köln: Kölnischer Kunstverein, 1970

– **Source. Music of the Avant-Garde** 11 (1974)

– **Tellus, The Audio Cassette Magazine** 24 (1990). Audio cassette tape. „FluxTellus"

– Van Toorn, Jan, ed. **Fluxus Anthology. 30th Anniversary. 1962–1992. Sound Events.** Den Bosch 1993

– Vautier, Ben, and Gino Di Maggio, eds. **Fluxus International & Co.** exh. cat. Liège: Ville de Liège; Milano: Multhipla; and Nice: Direction des Musées de Nice Action Culturelle Municipale, 1979

– **Visible Language** 26, no. 1–2 (Winter–Spring 1992). „Fluxus – A Conceptual Country"

– **Whitewalls: A Magazine of Writings by Artists** 16 (Spring 1987). „Fluxus"

– Wilhelm, Jean-Pierre, Nam June Paik, Wolf Vostell, and C. Caspari. „Magnum-Interview: Die Fluxus-Leute." Interviewers John Thwaites, Gottfried Michael Koenig, and Wolfgang Ramsbott. **Magnum,** no. 47 (April 1963): pp. 32–35, 62, 64, 66–68

– Williams, Emmett. **My Life in Flux – and Vice Versa.** Stuttgart: Edition Hansjörg Mayer, 1991